LEADERSHIP IN ACTION

INFLUENTIAL IRISH WOMEN NURSES' CONTRIBUTION TO SOCIETY

Edited by
Geraldine McCarthy and Joyce J. Fitzpatrick

Published by OAK TREE PRESS, 19 Rutland Street, Cork, Ireland
www.oaktreepress.com

A catalogue record of this book is available from the British Library.

ISBN 978 1 78119 029 6 (Paperback)
ISBN 978 1 78119 030 2 (ePub)
ISBN 978 1 78119 031 9 (Kindle)

CONTENTS

PREFACE

This book is both a testimony to the 20 Irish women who made a difference in society through their significant leadership contributions, and a book that can be used to teach aspiring leaders. We were inspired to write this book as we noticed frequent accounts in the media about women leaders who had begun their careers as nurses and went forward to make outstanding contributions in many aspects of Irish society, including the political and social service arenas. As nurse academics who have dedicated our careers to developing future leaders within the profession, we were in awe of those leaders who had made their mark outside of and within the profession. Thus we believe that not only students in nursing, but also future leaders in other disciplines, should learn from these powerful women leaders.

We chose to profile the women leaders because we believe the societal stereotype of nursing as a subservient women's profession is still strong. We wanted to directly address the 'double glass ceiling' that we believe many women in nursing face – that is, restrictions from both society and from the dominant medical profession. In particular, we want to encourage young leaders to chart new courses in their life's work and to build on the holistic, caring, interpersonal skills that are at the core of their nursing preparation.

We wish to acknowledge the women who were interviewed for these chapters, who gave generously of their time and energy. We are confident that their leadership profiles, their stories of success, and their advice to aspiring leaders will have a ripple effect for generations to come.

We also acknowledge the chapter contributors, most of whom were new doctoral students in nursing, who undertook this project as one of their first assignments in a leadership class. At the time, they were uncertain where the journey would lead, but were willing to leap into their new role, charting the course as the first graduate students in a new professional doctorate in nursing in Ireland.

Geraldine McCarthy and Joyce J. Fitzpatrick (Editors)

CHAPTER 1
INTRODUCTION:
PERSPECTIVES ON LEADERSHIP

Geraldine McCarthy and Joyce J. Fitzpatrick

Leadership is a familiar topic in management and professional courses. Theoretical and practical perspectives on leadership abound. From a review of internet sites, one can easily find a wide range of continuing education and self-help programmes designed to help individuals to gain beginning and advanced leadership skills.

Leadership courses frequently are embedded in academic and professional degree programmes. As academics, we have taught leadership to hundreds of students. A kaleidoscopic view of leadership theories that are predominant in health sciences programmes include transactional and transformational models, principled-centred leadership, servant leadership, quantum leadership, situational leadership, and leadership practices.

One of the most important components in understanding leadership is assessing one's own values. Leaders and those who aspire to leadership should engage in self-assessment, not only to clarify their values but also to know what skills they currently possess and those that will require development and/or refinement. Through self-assessment exercises, leaders also can identify their competencies and determine the best fit in relation to prospective positions.

Career planning is also important for aspiring leaders. Building on their self-assessment, aspiring leaders can select mentors to help them to round out their skills and abilities. While not all leaders would identify mentors in their career development, most identify influential persons who helped to guide their careers. The American College of Healthcare Executives (ACHE) offers several resources for developing mentoring relationships, both for the leader who is serving as mentor as well as for the protégé (ACHE, 2011). These resources include basic guides about the value and benefits of mentoring, the basics of mentoring relationships, and the creation of a career learning plan to extend beyond the mentoring relationship.

One of the most comprehensive perspectives on leadership that has dominated the leadership literature in the last decade is the work of Kouzes and Posner (2008). Over a period of 20 years, Kouzes and Posner gathered the views of 75,000 people to determine the common characteristics of leaders. The top five characteristics identified were honest, forward-looking, competent, inspiring, and intelligent. Kouzes and Posner then developed the five actions that they considered key to successful leadership: model the way; inspire a shared vision; challenge the process; enable others to act; and encourage the heart. Further, they developed the Leadership Practices Inventory (LPI), which can be used to assess these leadership characteristics. The LPI has been used in research across a range of disciplines; it also can be used as a self-assessment tool for aspiring leaders.

Another important leadership perspective is that of quantum leadership, developed by Porter-O'Grady and Malloch (2010). They identify key skills for leaders in nursing and healthcare; these include complexity, emotional competence, conflict management, and transformation skills. Further, these authors present a view that innovation should be a way of life for leaders. They also present key principles for the quantum leader (Malloch & Porter-O'Grady, 2009). These include: viewing the organisation as a complex mosaic; creating the broadest possible vision; managing information and dynamics; understanding the uncertainty and paradox of transformation; understanding both the formal and informal networks; and understanding the most important part of systems as their intersections (Malloch & Porter-O'Grady, pp. 1-19).

In learning to lead, individuals must build networks and coalitions. They must understand the flow of the organisations in which they work, and the need for interfaces with the many others who also are part of the organisation, including those within the formal and informal networks.

In summary, a number of models exist that describe and predict leadership characteristics and behaviours. In the following chapters, the contributors developed profiles of Irish women who have contributed to society and health, having begun their careers as clinical nurses. Each of the profiles includes the early influences and major life events that shaped the leader; the person's vision for their life work; their competencies, strengths and values; the significant challenges that they experienced; opportunities that enhanced their success; their perspective on the characteristics of leaders; and their advice to aspiring leaders. Importantly, these profiles provide a snapshot in time of the significant contributions of these leaders.

REFERENCES

American College of Healthcare Executives (2011). *Career Resource Center: Leadership in Mentoring.* Accessed 8 December 2011 from http://www.ache.org/newclub/career/MentorArticles/Mentoring.cfm.

Kouzes, J.M. & Posner, B.Z. (2008). *The Leadership Challenge* (4th ed.), San Francisco, CA: Jossey-Bass.

Malloch, K. & Porter-O'Grady, T. (2009). *The Quantum Leader: Applications for the New World of Work* (2nd ed.), Massachusetts: Jones & Bartlett.

Porter-O'Grady, T. & Malloch, K. (2010). *Quantum Leadership* (3rd ed.), Massachusetts: Jones & Bartlett.

CHAPTER 2
ELIZABETH ADAMS

Patrick Cotter

Do not underestimate people's talents, abilities and skills.

Elizabeth Adams is a Consultant, Nursing & Health Policy with the International Council of Nurses in Geneva, Switzerland. In addition, she is an Adjunct Associate Professor with Curtin University of Technology, Western Australia. She holds a

Bachelor's degree from University College Dublin and a Master's degree in Nursing from Trinity College Dublin.

She has previously held posts as Deputy Nursing Services Director, Health Service Executive, Ireland; Principal Nursing Officer, Department of Health, Western Australia; and Nurse Research Officer at the Office of the Chief Nursing Officer, Department of Health & Children, Ireland. In Western Australia, Elizabeth was involved in the introduction of advanced nursing practice, for which she received the Government of Western Australia's Recognition Award for Excellence in 2009.

Elizabeth's areas of expertise include positive practice environments, workforce planning, strategy and policy development. She has presented and published in these and other areas, including nurse prescribing and advanced nursing practice. Through her various positions, she has had the opportunity to work with a number of national, European and international organisations.

EARLY INFLUENCES

Elizabeth identified her family as being the major early influence on her life and career. Eileen, Elizabeth's paternal grandmother, was mother to 15 children and was described as a resourceful and innovative woman. May, Elizabeth's maternal grandmother, had suffered significant health problems but, despite this, displayed both pride and resilience throughout her life. According to Elizabeth, it was a 'privilege' to have these women in her life.

Her father, who worked for 49 years before retiring, also was a significant influence. Both of Elizabeth's parents were very family-focused, directing all of their resources into their three daughters. Her parents encouraged all of their children to learn both music and dance; Elizabeth learned to play a number of musical instruments as well as learning dance. She felt that it was her parents' goal that their three daughters would develop into well-rounded individuals.

Elizabeth's mother valued independence and prepared her daughters to be independent in life. Elizabeth described herself as shy but felt that her parents did not allow her to wallow in that shyness but encouraged her to function to her full potential in both life and work.

Elizabeth is the middle child of the three daughters. She describes her elder sister as having an incredible imagination, one she shared with Elizabeth as a child. She described her younger sister as living life to the fullest and for the moment; she grabs hold of opportunities as they arise.

MAJOR LIFE EVENTS

One of the most significant events in Elizabeth's life was being accepted into nursing.

The influence of one nursing sister on Elizabeth's practice, and ultimately her nursing path and leadership approach, is fondly remembered. From this experience, she developed an understanding of how impressionable young nurses are. She remembers how as a young nurse she worked with a ward sister who created a clear picture of expectations of staff. As a young nurse, she was empowered to care for patients. She believes that new nurses and midwives are the future of nursing and midwifery and feels that we must invest in creating for them a clear vision for the future of the professions.

Elizabeth was influenced by the many senior nursing staff with whom she worked. She believes that they demonstrated professionalism and knew how to communicate effectively with the entire healthcare team. She places great importance on the value of senior members of the nursing and midwifery team, as she believes that these are the people who have developed and built many of the services that we have in healthcare today. She has learned that people are the most important factor in patient care and that the interaction within and between the healthcare team is dependent on people, with nurses and midwives, more often than not, in a central and pivotal role. Elizabeth believes in multigenerational nursing teams where there is a healthy composition of both senior and junior nursing staff, all contributing to patient care and the development of the nursing profession.

Elizabeth recounted a number of traumatic events that have influenced her throughout her career, including working with patients following multiple traumas. These events emphasised the importance of being a skilled practitioner.

VISION FOR YOUR LIFE'S WORK

Elizabeth's vision for her life's work is to make a difference in the nursing and midwifery professions, especially in the area of clinical care through her work in policy development for nursing and midwifery, not only locally but also globally. Her vision is ultimately to affect a change in the care delivered to patients and their families.

She believes that nurses and midwives need to move towards the centre of health policy development and should be able to speak in unity on issues affecting their professions as well as on the future evolution and development of the professions. She believes that there are no other health professionals who are better positioned or prepared for this work.

COMPETENCIES, STRENGTHS AND VALUES

Elizabeth identifies an ability to understand the socio-political environment and the clinical environment as a strength. Her ability to communicate, she believes, has allowed her to develop positive relationships not only across the professions but also with global organisations such as the World Health Organization and the World Bank. Competence, in terms of communication and socio-political awareness, has enabled her to demonstrate to these groups the full potential of the nursing and midwifery professions.

Elizabeth also highlighted her ability to act ethically in all of her interactions with others, which she believes is essential in building and maintaining relationships. Learning from experience and using this in new situations, being able to adapt readily and having a people focus also are important strengths.

Elizabeth believes that the most important resource in healthcare is the people who work in frontline care services.

Elizabeth defined her own qualities as confident, trustworthy, positive, tolerant, analytical and committed. She believes that the leader needs to be confident and to set the direction for the followers. She believes her capacity for tolerance allows her to be accepting of others' ways of doing things. She also believes that one of her strongest qualities is commitment; she is committed to delivering excellence in all that she does.

Values espoused by Elizabeth include competence; understanding individuality; equality; responsibility; respect; dedication; diversity; loyalty; honesty; credibility; generosity; and empowerment.

CHARACTERISTICS OF LEADERS

To be visionary; have an ability to create ideas and give direction; be inspirational; define goals; and plan direction.

Leaders should use their leverage to achieve the goals of the group as well as assisting the members of the group in their work. The leader should be able to identify, nurture and develop the capabilities of others, allowing and facilitating the realisation of their abilities.

SIGNIFICANT CHALLENGES

Having spent 17 years working in clinical practice, Elizabeth described her move into the Department of Health & Children in Ireland as the most significant challenge in her career. The nature of work in policy development was quite different to what she had become used to in clinical practice. Another significant challenge was the implementation of policy initiatives – for example, the introduction of Nurse Practitioners in Western Australia (in which she had a leading role).

The experience and learning that Elizabeth gained from her involvement in this influenced her subsequent work. For example, she had a lead role in the introduction of nurse and midwife prescribing in Ireland for which legislation and practice changes in nursing and doctor roles was necessary. Elizabeth believes that the lessons learned, particularly those from Australia, shaped her and her team's approach to implementing this important initiative in nursing practice in Ireland.

OPPORTUNITIES THAT ENHANCED SUCCESS

One of the most significant opportunities that Elizabeth availed of was to do something different when her contract with the Department of Health & Children ended. She decided to take some time out and travel to Australia without any set plan in place. Prior to travelling, she had met with senior nurses from the Department of Health in Western Australia when they visited Ireland. They were interested in her work in manpower planning. Within a few days of arriving in Australia, she was asked by the Chief Nurse's Office in Western Australia to present her manpower research and subsequently was offered the opportunity to work with the Office of the Chief Nurse to develop and implement the role of the Nurse Practitioner in Western Australia. This opportunity, according to Elizabeth, is reflective of other opportunities that she has been open to throughout her career.

She says she is not particularly ambitious but has been open to, and taken, opportunities as they have presented themselves. She does not believe that individuals should have a definitive five-year plan as it could be restrictive and lead to refusal to consider opportunities as they arise.

OBSTACLES ENCOUNTERED AND LESSONS LEARNED

Elizabeth revealed that the biggest lesson that she has learned is to be absolutely inclusive. She believes that she has learned the importance of involving as many people as possible from the very beginning of any project or initiative. She has learned that others have alternative perspectives and opinions that deserve to be listened to and addressed through acknowledgement and discussion.

Mistakes have been a rich source of learning for Elizabeth. She feels that, through mistakes, she has had the opportunity to improve and develop as a nurse in both practice and policy development. She places emphasis on the importance of sharing the learning from mistakes with others.

Achieving a balance between work and home life is a challenge and ensuring that personal life is not subservient to her work life is difficult. She believes that she needs to learn how to achieve a better balance between life and work but it is a skill that is proving difficult to master.

ADVICE TO ASPIRING LEADERS

Do not underestimate people's talents, abilities and skills; do not have any boundaries; be open to ideas; and take advantage of opportunities as presented.

The key is to harness the existing talent and direct it into developing the profession, caring for patients and communities.

Aspiring leaders should have resilience and should not be afraid to take power and use it. Elizabeth believes that nurse leaders need to rebalance healthcare, where nurses and midwives have more influence over health policy.

CHAPTER 3
MARY BANOTTI

Patricia Fehin

*I have been extremely lucky in meeting and being
influenced by some quite exceptional people, but then
I suppose I went looking for them.*

Mary Banotti is a former Member of the European Parliament
(MEP) (1984 to 2004). She is currently the Honorary President of
Health First Europe, a member of the International Centre for

Missing and Exploited Children and has been Patron of the All Ireland Gerontological Nurses Association (AIGNA) since its establishment in 2009.

Mary left Ireland in the 1950s to train as a general nurse in London. She subsequently worked as a Registered Nurse in the United States, Canada, England, Italy and Africa. While in Africa, she was recruited to give mass anti-measles vaccinations; it was here that she developed her lifelong interest in issues in the developing world.

Mary returned to Ireland in 1970 to work as an occupational health nurse, and later, an industrial welfare officer within the Irish distilling industry. The 1970s represented a transitional stage in Irish life in which the women's liberation movement was at its infancy. Mary became actively involved in a number of campaigns, including the setting up of the first refuge for women experiencing domestic violence and facilities for better treatment for alcoholism. She campaigned to change inequalities in Irish family law.

Public service and politics are an inherent part of Mary Banotti's life. Mary is a grandniece of Irish patriot Michael Collins, and her sister Nora Owen, is a former Minister for Justice in the Irish Government.

Mary Banotti has been a prominent, respected elected official in Ireland. She ran for election to the Senate in 1982, for a Dáil by-election in 1983 and was elected to the European Parliament in 1984. She was narrowly defeated in the 1997 race to become the President of Ireland, finishing a strong second in a multi-candidate field. As a Member of the European Parliament, Mary worked on a variety of issues, including environmental and women's rights, and served as the European Parliament President's Mediator for Transnationally Abducted Children.

EARLY INFLUENCES

Mary grew up with her widowed mother and knew there was an expectation that each member of the family (her mother had six children under the age of 10 when her father died) would succeed in life. There was an absolute belief that every one of the children would receive appropriate training and education. Of her siblings, two are lawyers, one has a science degree and another has a successful career in industry. If her mother had not had a profession to fall back on, her children would have been put into care.

Mary's mother was a domestic science teacher. Her maternal grandfather believed everyone should have a profession or trade. He offered Mary's mother the opportunity to study law but she refused the offer, stating that no one would consult a woman solicitor. Ironically, when she died, the then President of the High Court and the Minister for Justice (her daughter, Nora Owen) were at her funeral. On the day she was buried, Garrett FitzGerald (leader of the Fine Gael political party) said the occasion was a 'celebration of gallant widows'. Mary herself says widows can be tough to live with but they are great role models.

Mary's mother was hugely influential in her life. While Mary initially wanted to be an actress, her mother encouraged her to study and achieve a qualification first. She worked initially in the National Irish Bank and, at just 18 years of age, left home to commence training as a nurse in England. Subsequently, Mary went to drama school in New York and had a minor career in acting there. Acting training was helpful in politics, particularly in relation to making presentations in the European Parliament.

Two particular teachers at the Dominican Convent School in Wicklow were influential in Mary's life. Sister Magdaline was a sophisticated woman for her time – a woman of the world with strong expectations of students and high standards. Sister Adrian was an intellectual who valued learning and communicated that to all her students.

Nursing was Mary's first exposure to women who were 'bosses' and she found that some were better than others in terms of how to get the maximum cooperation from less trained people. She quickly discerned who was good at leadership and why and who was bad and why.

MAJOR LIFE EVENTS

The death of her father was the first major life-changing event. It was a totally negative experience to a 10 year old who was the eldest of six children. Her father was a very funny man, an actor and a banker.

Other life influences were her sister's death and her own love affairs that did not last.

Mary says she is extremely proud of her nursing background and about how much she knows about nursing and medicine. This has been hugely beneficial to her, especially in the European Parliament on issues relating to health.

Mary worked in Canada where she was treated as a professional woman – this was totally different to how she had been treated in London as a student nurse. She remembers one reference she got from a nursing manager in Canada, which said, "Mary O'Mahony has a great many interesting aspects to her life which she brings to the benefit of her patients". She thinks a reference from the London training hospital might have stated that she was "not serious enough ... not a good nurse ...".

Mary was in the United States during the civil rights movement in the 1960s, just after President Kennedy was assassinated – an exciting and interesting time. She worked at Columbia Presbyterian Hospital in New York City. A number of people she met were politically active and she became politically active as well.

A major positive event was a trip to Kenya as part of a team to administer vaccinations for measles. In 1966, she worked in a hospital where there were huge advertisements for Pepsi Cola with pictures of Pepsi Cola being fed to a baby. Twenty years later, when she was a member of the European Parliament, a controversy developed about baby formula and the influence of the pharmaceutical industry in contrast to encouragement of breast-feeding. Her experience in Kenya made her comfortable about her perspective as she had seen firsthand how difficult it was for nursing staff in Kenya to promote healthy living in the face of advertising. Also, in Kenya, nurses were primarily medical assistants, usually men, with one year's training. This experience in Kenya helped her to focus her attention on the need for professional preparation of nurses and other medical personnel. Mary's experience as a nurse in the developing world also helped with other issues that arose in the European Parliament – for example, family planning and HIV/AIDS.

Mary returned to Ireland in 1970 after her marriage broke up and, with the challenge of bringing up a child alone, she got involved in the women's liberation movement. This involvement was precipitated by a feeling of how important it was and how few rights Irish women had.

VISION FOR YOUR LIFE'S WORK

Mary's vision was to give as much support as possible to women but to emphasise also that they have to learn to cope with failure.

She would like to be remembered as a good mother, an energetic and effective politician, and as someone who had overcome failure and difficulty enough to make a contribution to the life of her country.

COMPETENCIES, STRENGTHS AND VALUES

Mary described herself as intelligent, widely-read, courageous, a risk-taker, a good communicator, a clear thinker, and well-organised.

She holds respect for people, family and friends, and a belief in service. She believes that all have a responsibility to serve fellow human beings. She feels this commitment to others was an important characteristic of the Ireland she grew up with. Her belief in service continues, as she is involved in the community, with Meals on Wheels and as Chairperson of the Irish Centre for Abducted Children (a telephone helpline).

CHARACTERISTICS OF LEADERS

According to Mary, a leader is one who is intelligent; believes what they are doing is worthwhile and important; has a vocation for the post; is prepared to take responsibility and learn how to be effective; and is courageous, well-organised and well-informed.

SIGNIFICANT CHALLENGES

Being an insulin dependent diabetic (for 35 years) has brought challenges (including cardiac problems), which were resented initially but were managed and allowed Mary's election to public office. Back pain is a problem now, which initially developed while practicing nursing.

Dealing with prejudice (including racial) has been a challenge, as was waiting until her daughter was 15 years of age before entering politics. She found that any woman with a young family who enters political life must have an extremely supportive husband/partner/family. Mary pretended for a long time that it was all possible, but found that this was not the case. Rather the support of others was necessary.

OPPORTUNITIES THAT ENHANCED SUCCESS

Mary says that being born at the right time and being in Ireland at the right time were opportunities that enhanced her success. She also feels that she was lucky to have had a good education and training. In particular, nursing, which is an intrinsic part of what she is and does, prepared her for being resilient. For example, resilience is necessary when seeking a nomination to be a candidate for election in politics and, once elected, being determined to stay elected.

Fluency in Italian and French also provided opportunities and proved helpful in getting to know international colleagues in political life.

While in the European Parliament, Mary had the opportunity to volunteer and become a member of the Petitions Committee, which had a remit in relation to abducted children. Her own child had been abducted so she understood the issues involved. Child abduction was not a political issue at that time but she managed to make it one.

ADVICE TO ASPIRING LEADERS

Mary advises aspiring leaders to take risks; learn from failures; be realistic; appreciate your friends and family; embrace life; and be political.

CHAPTER 4
JOSEPHINE BARTLEY

Vicki Cleary

*I always felt that communication was very important, proper
communication and showing respect for people.*

Josephine Bartley is Acting Secretary General of the International
Catholic Committee of Nurses and Medico-Social Assistants. She
retired from her position as Director of Nursing at Beaumont
Hospital in 1998; she was appointed to this position in 1987,
following the amalgamation of Richmond Hospital and Jervis Street
Hospital.

She completed her general nurse training at St. Vincent's University Hospital, Dublin in 1955. Subsequently, she completed her midwifery training at the Royal Maternity Hospital in Belfast. In the following years, Josephine served with the Queen Alexandra's Royal Army Nursing Corps, before returning to London, where she worked as a midwife at Queen Charlotte's Maternity Hospital.

On her return to Ireland, Josephine took up a position as Assistant Director of Nursing at St. Vincent's University Hospital Dublin, before being appointed Director of Nursing of the Richmond Hospital, Dublin.

Despite retirement, Josephine still is very actively involved in the nursing profession. She serves on the Board of Directors of Our Lady's Children's Hospital, Crumlin, Dublin and is involved with the Nursing Faculty of the Royal College of Surgeons in Ireland.

EARLY INFLUENCES

Family was an important early influence for Josephine, who describes her sister as one of the most influential people in her choice of career. During her school years, Josephine wished to become a teacher. However, once her sister commenced her nurse training, Josephine made the decision to follow in her sister's footsteps. One of the main reasons for this change in direction was Josephine's wish to be close to her sister.

Other influential members of her family included Josephine's mother, who was very keen to have her children educated to ensure their financial security.

Another important influence was that of religion. Josephine reported that her decision to train at St. Vincent's Hospital, which was run by the Sisters of Charity, was influenced by the dominant religious background in her family. Religion was very important to Josephine and was an important source of strength during times of difficulty.

MAJOR LIFE EVENTS

Josephine states that certain personalities whom she encountered throughout her working life influenced her. She swore to herself when she entered nurse management that she would not behave like some of the Matrons she had encountered. She recalled nurse managers who were very hard on their staff and rarely listened to what their staff had to say. She promised herself that, when she became a manager, her personality would not change and she would not become hard. She swore that she would not become a dictator of any kind. Josephine describes her encounters with nurse managers such as these as a good thing, as it made her aware of the kind of leader she did not want to become.

VISION FOR YOUR LIFE'S WORK

Throughout Josephine's working life, she was very committed to the advancement of her career. Despite this, she reports that her entry into nurse management was by chance. She was invited to apply for her first management post and surmises that other people must have seen qualities in her that she could not see herself. It was this chance invitation that put her on the path to a post as Director of Nursing.

Once Josephine entered senior management positions, she described her vision as providing a good, safe, efficient service to patients. In particular, she recognised the importance of having a contented nursing staff and strove to achieve this throughout her time in leadership. She describes this as a simple, yet important, vision. To achieve this, she instigated a change in management structures within the hospital to make it easier for all staff to know to whom they were accountable. She hopes that she achieved her vision but recognises the importance of not being too soft when in a leadership position.

COMPETENCIES, STRENGTHS AND VALUES

Josephine acknowledges that her interpersonal relations skills are a major strength, to which she attributes to the success of her career. She concedes that she was very particular about all aspects of communication, including the writing of letters, to the extent that she would not put her signature on a letter that was not absolutely perfect.

Josephine believes proper communication and demonstrating respect for people are of utmost importance within a leadership position. She endeavoured to solve any grievances with staff quickly, without holding a grudge. She also recognised the importance of taking advice from others, especially those who had the best interests of the organisation at heart.

Josephine considers that her work was based on values such as honesty and fairness. She believes these values were instilled in her through her up-bringing at home and through her education.

CHARACTERISTICS OF LEADERS

First, Josephine believes it is essential to lead by example. She proposes that, to be a good leader, you must lead by example.

She feels it is necessary to demonstrate respect to all those you work with to ensure cooperation. Being a good team player, a good listener and having the ability to delegate efficiently are other characteristics she believes are necessary to be a good leader. She considers that leaders should be calm, kind and knowledgeable.

She also proposes that some people have innate characteristics that make them good leaders.

SIGNIFICANT CHALLENGES

Josephine compared nurse training in her time to entering a convent but yet she considered the experience worthwhile.

The most significant challenges during her career were her involvement in the relocation of two hospitals. First, during her time as Assistant Director of Nursing at St. Vincent's Hospital, Dublin, she was involved with the hospital's relocation to another site within the city. Similarly, during her appointment as Director of Nursing of the Richmond Hospital, she was involved in the amalgamation of this hospital with Jervis Street Hospital to become the newly-formed Beaumont Hospital, in which she retained her Director of Nursing post.

These two events posed similar challenges. Not only was the logistics of transferring patients a significant challenge, but the settling in of staff posed a considerable obstacle. In particular, the amalgamation of staff from two separate organisations was a substantial challenge that had to be overcome. Josephine recalls the difficulty of trying to assign staff to wards that corresponded with the areas they previously worked in to ensure an adequate skill mix. Although Josephine acknowledges that everything worked out reasonably well, she reported that organisational problems were further compounded by staff shortages and lack of funding. Financial difficulties hindered the recruitment of staff, which put considerable strain on the organisation as a whole.

OPPORTUNITIES THAT ENHANCED SUCCESS

Josephine attributes much of her success to the people she encountered throughout her career. She believes she was very lucky to have encountered such good staff who supported her during difficult times. During her appointment as Director of Nursing at Beaumont Hospital, she acknowledges that she was very fortunate to have met many people who had progressive ideas that helped to move the organisation forward. She believes that, without the help of these progressive thinkers, the organisation would not have prospered.

Josephine endeavoured to build a strong relationship with the Schools of Nursing. She believes that this relationship enhanced her success as it was beneficial to seek advice on matters from outside the hospital environment.

OBSTACLES ENCOUNTERED AND LESSONS LEARNED

Josephine could not recollect any particular obstacle that she encountered throughout her career. However, she reveals that dealing with difficult people posed significant obstacles on more than one occasion. Josephine often questioned whether she was being fair with people during these encounters and often sought advice from the human resources department. She quickly learned that you had to have a thick skin and not to give in to people if you knew you were right. She learned to trust her own knowledge and her own integrity. However, she acknowledges that this was not easy and she would question herself endlessly.

ADVICE TO ASPIRING LEADERS

Respect your staff and treat them fairly; be generous with your time; and show respect.

She appeals to future Directors of Nursing and people in leadership positions to "respect nurses, to appreciate their staff and treat them kindly and have the courage to persist in what you believe".

CHAPTER 5
CECILY BEGLEY

Elizabeth Heffernan

*It is that kind of persistence going back again and again until
you achieve whatever it is that is important.*

Cecily Begley is the founding Professor of Nursing & Midwifery at
Trinity College Dublin (TCD), having been appointed to that post
in 2004.

Following four years in general nursing, and 12 years as a
midwife, nurse tutor and research fellow in the Coombe Hospital,

Dublin, in 1989 Cecily became a Lecturer, then Senior Lecturer, in the Faculty of Nursing, Royal College of Surgeons in Ireland (RCSI). In 1996, she took up the post of the Director of the School of Nursing & Midwifery at TCD and was charged with the task of developing a new School.

She was a ministerial appointment to the Nursing Education Forum, the National Implementation Committee for undergraduate BSc nurse education, and the Expert Group and National Implementation Committee direct entry programmes in Midwifery and Children's Nurse Education. Overseas, she was involved in collaboration with Queen's University, Belfast in providing consultancy services to the University of Jordan in developing and modernising its MSc nursing programmes.

Cecily has secured substantial research funding and has published widely on physiological childbirth and women-centred care; maternal morbidity; self-esteem and assertiveness in student nurses and midwives. She is a reviewer and member of the editorial boards of a number of journals and provides supervision and external examining of PhD/ MSc by research students.

EARLY INFLUENCES

An early influence on Cecily was her father's death when she was eight years old. Her mother then had to work full-time, which was very unusual at that time. Her mother also cared for Cecily's grandparents (her father's parents) until they died; then her mother cared for her own father at home. As a result, Cecily feels that she grew up to be very self-sufficient and was influenced by her mother's ethos of hard work and caring attitude.

She has various relatives who are doctors or physiotherapists, and initially she had no desire to become a nurse – in fact, mathematics was her first choice of career. Both her parents were mathematics teachers and she was preparing to study in TCD to undertake a degree in mathematics. Just months before she left school, she realised she wanted to work with people and thus choose nursing/midwifery as a career.

MAJOR LIFE EVENTS

One of the people who influenced Cecily in nursing was her very first ward sister. Then a year or so later, this ward sister got married; she left nursing because the law at the time did not allow women to work in a permanent position after marriage. This ward sister returned to work two years later in a temporary capacity when Cecily was as a third year student nurse and the assumption was that Cecily was in a post more senior than the returning nurse. This incident was seen as unjust for Irish society as a whole and for nursing in particular, as nurses could lose their value so quickly by doing something as simple as getting married.

Another person who influenced her career was a night sister who saved a man's life one night when the doctors were unsure of what to do. These and many other events taught her how experienced nurses can be so very important in the health service.

Another influence was when she moved outside of clinical nursing and enrolled in the Diploma in Nursing at University College Dublin (UCD). Judith Chavasse co-ordinated the course and Cecily learned a tremendous amount from her as she provided theory on research methodology and opened Cecily's eyes to research possibilities, which endured over time.

VISION FOR YOUR LIFE'S WORK

Cecily worked in clinical nursing and in midwifery for 12 years before she moved fully into third-level education. She never really thought out her career trajectory but took opportunities as they arose.

She loved teaching but, after being exposed to research during study for the Diploma from UCD, she discovered how wonderful it was to find an answer to a question through research that could improve clinical practice. This set her on a research road, which continues to the present.

Cecily was part of the movement in Ireland to transfer nursing and midwifery training into third-level education, which culminated in the establishment of the Commission on Nursing in 1996. The Commission's recommendations led to the introduction of a BSc degree for all students entering nursing and the establishment of clinical and managerial career pathways within nursing/midwifery.

Once nursing moved into third level, Cecily was focused immediately on developing a strategy for education/research at varying levels for nurses and midwives. Also she has a vision to make maternity care in Ireland women-centred, because she perceives it as not focused on women at the present time.

COMPETENCIES, STRENGTHS AND VALUES

Cecily is a committed educator and firmly believes in nurses/midwives having degree-level education.

Her main strength is that she is a very hard worker. She has persistence, going back again and again until she achieves whatever is important, and she succeeds because she just keeps working hard. She also thinks having a positive outlook and expecting the best of everybody and expecting that everything will turn out right is really important.

CHARACTERISTICS OF LEADERS

Leaders should be inspirational; interested; motivational; enthusiastic; supportive; and encouraging.

They should praise and facilitate people in whatever they are doing. To be educated and knowledgeable are also characteristics of leaders.

SIGNIFICANT CHALLENGES

When she moved into third level, in her first position she was the sole academic and found it challenging because she had no support or colleagues for discussion purposes. Also, nurses in senior posts held management positions but did not understand either nursing or education within academia. In having discussions and debates on issues and trying to persuade people on her vision, she learned a great deal.

Other challenges included juggling the demands of a challenging academic position with the need to spend time with her husband and three children; and dealing with the fact that 10 friends and family close to her died in a very short space of time.

Challenges at the moment include those associated with the economic recession which is affecting everybody.

Cecily feels that we must learn new methods of working and concentrate on important things. She suggests we get rid of many meetings and much of the associated documentation. Instead, we should concentrate on people and ask ourselves questions such as: Are we educating the students correctly? Are we looking after the patients' rights?

OPPORTUNITIES THAT ENHANCED SUCCESS

Cecily states that the first opportunity that enhanced her success was her admission to the Diploma in UCD. A clinical issue of concern led to the opportunity to write a research proposal and achieve funding to undertake research for a Master's degree by research on the appropriate use of Ergometrine.

Other opportunities included the appointment as Lecturer, then Senior Lecturer, in the Faculty of Nursing at the RCSI (at that time, it was one of only two colleges offering nurse education programmes). She spent eight years developing programmes and it was an incredible learning curve. The opportunity to establish a

School of Nursing and research within Trinity College Dublin provides further career success for Cecily.

OBSTACLES ENCOUNTERED AND LESSONS LEARNED

Cecily thinks her biggest mistake in the early days was not involving other people enough, as she was afraid of overworking or exhausting them and that they would not be able to cope. She now knows that this is actually quite denigrating to people and perhaps provided obstacles to their advancement. The lesson learned was to improve communication, and explain in as much detail as possible the way ahead rather than assuming everybody understood the importance of what was to be done.

She also learned to never get upset or disheartened by obstacles placed in your path – just learn from it and move on quickly.

ADVICE TO ASPIRING LEADERS

Work hard; listen to people; take every opportunity arising; learn to control emotions; delegate based on competencies; and support, educate and develop team members.

When leading a team, facilitate team members; learn and practice better ways of interacting with people; try and understand what they are talking about; trust them; promote a win-win perspective; delegate within competence and mentor, but help where necessary.

Use lots of praise every time something goes right. When things go wrong, try and find out what happened and what remedies are required (mentoring, learning from the mistake, etc) so that it does not happen again.

You succeed in supporting your team to succeed, because it is actually they who create the success.

CHAPTER 6
ANNE CARRIGY

Irene O'Connor

Go for it; do not stand back; put your hand up.

Anne Carrigy is President of An Bord Altranais. She trained as a nurse in Dublin and has held many posts within the Irish health services, including: National Lead for Acute Hospital Services, Health Service Executive (HSE) in Ireland (2008 to 2010); Director of Nursing at the Mater Hospital, Dublin (1998 to 2008); Head of Corporate Affairs, Mater Hospital, Dublin (2005).

Anne thinks her diverse nursing experience was an excellent preparation and sound basis for the nationally-focused roles she has held within an evolving health service. She was appointed by the Minister for Health to the Board of the Medical Council of Ireland (2008). She is a member of Sigma Theta Tau International Honour Society of Nursing (Rho Chi Chapter, University of Utrecht, Netherlands) since 2004 and was President of the European Federation of Nursing Professions (2009) and President of the European Council of Nursing Regulators (FEPI). Anne was conferred as an Honorary Fellow of the Faculty of Nursing & Midwifery, Royal College of Surgeons Ireland (2007) and appointed Adjunct Associate Professor, Department of Nursing Studies, University College Dublin (2010).

EARLY INFLUENCES

Three women influenced Anne's life and career. Anne's mother, who continues to live independently in her 92nd year, a woman of farming background and having herself an unfulfilled desire to become a nurse, continues to be a great support. Anne commenced her career in nursing in August 1966 in the Mater Hospital, Dublin, at the age of 17. Career choices for women were limited at the time and Anne desired a career with a practical dimension. Thus the career choice was either training as a domestic science teacher or as a nurse.

Sister Concepta, Matron of the Mater Hospital, was the second woman to influence Anne's nursing and leadership career. Anne recalls her as a person of great expertise and, in particular, she was great with people. Anne describes Sister Concepta as having an amazing skill to turn difficult experiences into learning opportunities. The Sisters of Mercy have influenced Anne through their major contribution to healthcare in Ireland. Anne views her years in training as a nurse as offering opportunities and mentoring by expert nurses in both clinical and teaching positions. The enjoyment she was exposed to in the development of her own clinical competencies also has remained with her.

Assistant Matron, Ms. Gilsenan, a woman of great integrity, strict but fair, who always sought high standards in patient care, was the third person to have a great impact on Anne. Anne believed the skill sets learned in intensive care nursing gave her the grounding for leadership and management. The experience in intensive care nursing of dealing constantly with challenging and very difficult situations and working within a multidisciplinary team in a multispecialty environment was influential in Anne's career development.

Anne took time out of her career when she married and had three children. During this time, she worked with her father in a private company, where she learned the world of business.

VISION FOR YOUR LIFE'S WORK

For Anne, life always needs to be in a state of balance. She always leaves work at work. She describes herself as very organised; she plans her day, and gets to work always on time and early when the need arises.

She was not appointed when she first competed for senior posts. Anne thinks that frequently better opportunities come your way when the timing is right, but you have to be ready and available. Sister Lucy Therese, Director of Nursing, insisted on Anne giving attention to career planning. This led to availing herself of educational and professional development opportunities, the first being a ward sister's administration certificate in University College Dublin and culminating in an MSc in nursing.

Anne believes that a person should not hold a Director of Nursing position for longer than seven years, even though there may be no definite career pathway thereafter.

Anne at all times believed in the need for clinical governance and corporate governance to be an integrated model and welcomes very much the creation of the Office of National Clinical Director and Nursing within the Health Service Executive framework. Anne believes that greater vision and leadership in nursing is required to ensure effective contribution from nursing and nurses. Anne believes that a professorship in clinical nursing, based on the clinical site, is both desirable and necessary.

She always has enjoyed her career and her family and continues to enjoy both and her grandchildren.

COMPETENCIES, STRENGTHS AND VALUES

Anne believes that strength of character is essential for work in leadership and nursing. The dynamics of the work environment, including dealing with human and complex issues, requires the ability to shift one's perspectives, adjust to changing dynamics, lead staff, and both take and manage risks. Her passion for her current role originated from her experience as a nurse providing direct care.

She wonders whether caring is a characteristic one is born with or learns. She believes one has to be a caring person to enter nursing and then build on this through experience. Anne views nursing as challenging. The type of work and the human dilemmas experienced call for a moral and ethical approach. Fairness, openness and doing the right thing by people require strength of character. In addition, staff issues are complex but Anne always felt competent and confident to address the issues presented.

She constantly refers back to her training experience as the genesis of learning the competencies gained. Anne sees the new model of nurse education and training as a very positive development.

Anne's pride in being a nurse is exemplified in her understanding of nursing as a privileged career, being the only professional with 24-hour contact with patients, seven days a week, 52 weeks of the year. As a graduate of the first programme of intensive care nursing organised in Ireland in 1970, Anne values the needs of patients and families in times of great distress. She views the role of the nurse as one of leadership and coordination, along with direct care-giver, whichever the circumstances require. The 24/7 exposure and knowledge places the nurse in a unique position as all other clinicians 'step in and step out' of the whole patient experience. She feels that nurses do not articulate well what nurses do.

CHARACTERISTICS OF LEADERS

Anne identifies being a listener and a mentor as core traits of leadership. She emphasises insight, strength of character, good communication skills, respect for self and others and the maintenance of confidentiality as necessary requirements for leaders. Upholding the dignity of the person, through being respectful and trusting, and how one speaks to others is of great importance.

Insight, Anne explains, is having the ability to be accommodating in one's thinking and views, describing no situation as black and white. This does not mean or necessitate dropping one's standards.

Leadership requires the ability to guide, persuade, bring people along, bestow confidence in staff and direct when required. It means not asking others to do what you would not be prepared to do yourself or that which is outside their level of competence.

SIGNIFICANT CHALLENGES

The 'Stardust' experience (a large fire in a nightclub in Dublin in 1981 involving many victims) was a very real challenge for Anne as a nurse and one she recalls as proving a major learning experience in clinical care and management.

Anne views the delivery of direct clinical care as the most challenging and stressful of all in nursing. To manage and lead others, Anne sees as requiring people to step back and remove personalities from decisions. This can result in people thinking one is 'hard' but emotions can interfere with good decisions.

Health service and nursing leadership is very public, yet patient issues are very private. Traumatic experiences for the patient and, in particular, death of a young person is very stressful for staff.

At executive level, the challenge of protecting the delivery of quality patient care *versus* the delivery of organisational goals can be onerous. Nurse leaders must be effective in informing and influencing decisions. Objectivity is required when prioritising decisions, while understanding other people's agendas and recognising one's own biases.

The necessity of overseas recruitment of nurses in the 1990s, when there were staff shortages, posed many challenges for leaders in nursing. It required the creation of a very dynamic work environment and an understanding of people from different cultures.

Anne also considers maintaining a work-life balance as a constant challenge.

OPPORTUNITIES THAT ENHANCED SUCCESS

Anne views educational and professional opportunities as important. Anne enjoyed her work all her life, no two days were the same, one could never describe the job of nursing as 'humdrum' and opportunities did arise.

When promotional opportunities presented, the support from her family was very important in enabling her to compete for the positions and become a member of bodies as requested. The exposure she got as a member of varying committees in the Department of Health & Children, University College Dublin and An Bord Altranais broadened her knowledge and networks.

Even though she was contemplating retirement, an opportunity in the Health Service Executive (HSE) in the management of adverse incidents presented a specific area of interest and challenge.

Secondment fulltime to the HSE during the change process gave Anne an opportunity to step out of nursing and to gain insight into the HSE and the broader perspective of healthcare delivery. A subsequent opportunity in the position of National Lead in Acute Hospital Services presented and she was appointed to the position. She believes that her experience grounded in nursing placed her in an ideal position for this post and associated responsibilities.

Anne views most things as cyclical in nature; having her experience in acute services, opportunism and readiness placed Anne in the position to lead in her current role.

OBSTACLES ENCOUNTERED AND LESSONS LEARNED

Anne always liked to aim high. Such an approach can bring elements of frustration, but Anne's attitude is that, when one door closes, another opens. Anne did not always succeed when applying for promotion but something much better always turned up.

Management of people can be difficult but is a skill that one develops over time and with experience.

Anne acknowledged that she must have made mistakes in her career – for example, not becoming a midwife, though successful in obtaining a midwifery training position, remains a 'niggling thing' for her.

Travel Anne sees as an opportunity for all young nurses and one to be availed of to gain experience of life and nursing.

Anne feels very privileged and proud to be a nurse, describing it as a wonderful career with great job satisfaction. She values the opportunities that her nursing career has brought to her as a person from a professional perspective and the lifelong friends on a personal level.

ADVICE TO ASPIRING LEADERS

Anne recommends that one should go for it. Do not stand back, rather put your hand up ... if leadership is your ambition.

She emphasises that a leader needs to be sensitive to others. According to Anne, "... future leaders must present themselves and take the opportunities available, while simultaneously creating opportunities for others".

CHAPTER 7
NORAH CASEY

Josephine Hegarty

Time was an enormous challenge, I think. Because of my absolute fundamental belief in learning, it's not something I have ever been willing to sacrifice.

Norah Casey is Chief Executive Officer (CEO) and the owner of Harmonia Ltd., which assumed the business of Smurfit Communications in August 2004. Dublin-based, Harmonia has a strong portfolio of brands and events in Ireland, the USA and more recently in China, and publishes a range of market-leading magazines. Norah is the newest Dragon in the Irish version of

Dragons' Den (2011). She is a member of the National Paediatric Hospital Development Board, the London-based Women's Irish Network and the International Women's Forum. She was awarded the *Veuve Clicquot Business Woman of the Year* award for 2007/8 and won the *Publisher of the Year* award in 2006, 2007 and 2008. Prior to 2004, Norah was CEO of Smurfit Communications, Smurfit Online Services, and Smurfit Media UK.

Before joining the Smurfit Group in May 1998, she was CEO of Scutari Press (later Royal College of Nursing Publishing), with a portfolio of 16 magazine titles, an event unit with over 100 conferences and exhibitions annually and a book publishing unit. Norah has edited numerous nursing journals, including *Nursing Standard* and *Evidence-Based Nursing*.

Norah trained as a general nurse in Scotland and undertook a Certificate in Burns & Plastic Surgery at Bangour Village Hospital, prior to moving to the Royal College of Nursing (RCN). She undertook a post-graduate print journalism course and subsequently gained qualifications in television production and radio journalism. She studied strategic management at Ashridge Management College in the UK, undertook a Smith & Nephew scholarship in the USA and registered for a PhD at the University of Wales in 1991.

She is widely published in periodical and book format and she has published her own book, *Images of Romania*, in 1991 (Scutari Press).

EARLY INFLUENCES

Norah Casey grew up in the Phoenix Park in Dublin, where her father was a Park Ranger. Despite the fact that both her mother and aunt were nurses, she had no early aspirations of becoming a nurse. She worked in Dublin Zoo from a young age and is proud of the fact that she helped to rear the first two baby gorillas there.

Norah was 17 years old and had completed her Leaving Certificate when she heard about a little hospital in Scotland that was recruiting for nurse trainees. The idea of escaping home appealed. She applied for a place, was interviewed and was accepted onto the three-year apprenticeship nursing training programme in The Vale of Leven District General Hospital, near Loch Lomond in West Scotland. Norah enjoyed the journey into nursing, the newness of leaving Ireland, being on a plane for the first time, without really thinking about the career path that she had chosen. Being the only non-Scottish person in the programme, she often was left in the nursing home on her own. Having all this extra time, she bought into the whole culture of nursing much more so than any of her colleagues. She was an avid reader, she got on really well with her lecturers and she devoured nursing theory. Norah travelled to different parts of Scotland from Loch Lomond to fulfil the various programme requirements. Norah was a very active member of the RCN, where she ran the student chapter. She found a great camaraderie with her RCN colleagues, enjoyed going to the meetings, linking with so many senior nurses, and organising seminars/lectures.

Norah loved nursing and noted the distinctiveness between nursing and medicine, their unique roles in the provision of care and the holistic approaches taken by nurses. However, from a healthcare perspective, she was frustrated with the bureaucracy and the difficulties she perceived in achieving what one wanted to achieve, the layers of management and the rules and the paraphernalia that sometimes masked the fact that you were trying to accomplish something important to the care of patients. During her student years, Norah was very politically aware; she was familiar with the writings of nursing theorists, the evolving nursing knowledge base and the beginning of the movement away from the apprenticeship model of nurse training to the education of nurses in a situation where students are extra to the work force.

In terms of major influences, Virginia Henderson had an enormous influence on Norah. She was particularly influenced by Henderson's early publications and articulation of the difference between nursing and medicine. Norah remembers reading the *Textbook of the Principles & Practice of Nursing* and *The Nature of*

Nursing, in which she thought Henderson encapsulated nursing beautifully. Virginia Henderson was quite an elderly woman when Norah eventually got to meet and interview her.

MAJOR LIFE EVENTS

Norah was 21 years old when she qualified as a nurse and she was a little nervous about practice. Instead of running away from this fear, she decided to complete a Certificate in Burns & Plastic Surgery at Bangour Village Hospital in West Lothian, Scotland. She spent a year there, and it was during this time that she decided that perhaps clinical nursing was not necessarily the right career choice for her. She described the programme as wonderful but also very intense, given the long shifts of one-to-one concentrated and individualised care.

A senior RCN colleague noticed that there was a vacancy in the RCN (London) for a Student Association Officer. Even though the lower age limit for application was 25 and she was only 23, she cheekily applied for the job anyway. Trevor Clay (General Secretary of the RCN, who subsequently became her mentor), was on the interview panel. Interestingly, the interview developed into a really good intellectual dialogue about nursing and where it was going and, despite all the odds, Norah got the job. This time in her career was transformative. Her salary was more than doubled, she had a car and a secretary and an office in the heart of London. Trevor Clay took Norah under his wing, as he set about changing the public's perception of nursing and the RCN (away from the twin-set and pearls image). Norah received intensive media training and she became the public persona of the RCN. Thus Norah became very comfortable in speaking publicly. Her job entailed talking to student groups, attending meetings, organising conferences and responding to media interview requests, as well as lecturing on nursing and RCN-related issues. Norah was fascinated by the public/political side of nursing and the fact that nursing was going through a period of transformation.

However, after two or three years, Norah needed a change. She did not want to go back to clinical nursing with the restrictions of working in a hospital environment. Her mentor (Trevor Clay) shepherded Norah into journalism and she began to work with the *Nursing Standard* (a weekly newspaper for nurses), while also writing for *The Guardian*. Given her new interests, Norah decided to take a postgraduate programme in journalism accredited by the National Council for the Training of Journalists in Harlow College and stayed working at the *Nursing Standard* as a news reporter. By now, she was both a Registered General Nurse and a qualified journalist. Very rapidly, Norah rose through the ranks, moving from News Reporter to News Editor and, eventually, Editor at the *Nursing Standard*.

At the time, the RCN wanted to set up a separate publishing company, called Scutari after the place where Florence Nightingale cared for victims of the Crimea. The plan was to create a new journal, a metamorphosis of the weekly newspaper (*Nursing Standard*) and to develop a whole stable of journals specifically for nurses. At that time, there was not much published material available in the UK or Europe aimed specifically at nurses. Norah became CEO of this wholly-owned subsidiary publishing company (later known as RCN Publishing).

During her time at the publishing company, Norah travelled the world, spending some time in the United States researching publishing. She was particularly interested in how they engaged in the process of awarding continuing education points for reading a particular article. In the UK, Norah was seconded to work for a short period of time to the United Kingdom Central Council to help develop what later became known as post-registration education and practice (PREP). She then was able to translate that work into something that was phenomenally successful – for example, when an individual read an article, they completed some multiple choice questions which then could be used to earn one or two hours of continuing education points.

By the time Norah left the company (in 1998), it had 16 magazines and journals and a significant conference programme.

From Norah's perspective, one of her greatest publishing achievements within this portfolio of journals was *Evidence-Based Nursing*, which was a joint publication with the *British Medical Journal* (BMJ), produced in liaison with the University of Toronto and the University of Oxford as a one-stop resource for the latest research across all nursing specialties. It took two years of collaborative work alongside Richard Smith (the then editor of the BMJ) and many others to peer-review, critique and distil a large amount of research into short journal articles, thus moving nursing practice one step further and encouraging further study. When Norah left RCN Publishing, she was presented with the first bound and signed volume of *Evidence-Based Nursing*, which still takes pride of place on her bookshelf.

In terms of key life lessons, Norah, as Head of Scutari (later RCN Publishing), realised the absolute joy she got out of running businesses. She could produce fantastic peer-reviewed journals, mass-produce consumer magazines and organise hundreds of conferences. However, she actually found greater professional satisfaction when she discovered a niche in the market, researched it, developed the budget and the business plan, launched it and discovered that it made a profit. An example of this was when Norah was studying for her Master's at the University of Wales and subsequently went on to study for her PhD with Bren Davis at the School of Nursing and discovered there was very little by way of materials for researchers. So she launched a journal called *Nurse Researcher*. Each issue had a particular research theme, and it turned out to be a phenomenal success, which she enjoyed very much.

Norah moved to the *Irish Post* newspaper, published by the Jefferson Smurfit Group under the banner of Smurfit Media UK. She enjoyed working there but, very quickly, the Smurfit Group asked her to run its Dublin magazine publishing company and its 'on-line' company in Dublin. The Smurfit Group made no secret of the fact that they considered the publishing activities in Ireland as non-core activities. Thus Norah knew that there was a possibility of a management buyout (MBO) and, in 2004, she did just that, becoming the owner and CEO of Harmonia Ltd, Ireland's largest magazine publishing company, printing over four million magazines annually for the Irish, British and US markets.

Currently, Norah is working in China. With the recent recession, she thinks that we could do more in the emerging markets. Norah took her family to do a study tour of Asia, Australia and New Zealand for four months. She met with over 30 publishers, and created a new business line. She notes that sometimes you just have to be brave enough to say, "I am not sitting around waiting for the next foot to fall".

In 2011, Norah became one of the Dragons on the *Dragons' Den* programme aired on Irish television. *Dragons' Den* is a reality television programme featuring entrepreneurs pitching their business ideas in order to secure investment finance from a panel of potential investors.

VISION FOR YOUR LIFE'S WORK

Norah says that her greatest publishing achievement was to launch *Evidence-Based Nursing*. However, letting go of nursing was another big moment in her life; it was very, very difficult for her to let go, close to a bereavement. RCN Publishing was her baby, she had helped create it, and she had developed and nurtured it. She could have stayed there for the rest of her life but although she was somewhat comforted by the fact that she might find herself there at retirement, part of her was slightly horrified. However, she chose to take a big risk and see where it would take her.

Within her professional life, the Harmonia MBO was her biggest accomplishment; she was transformed by that move. She now had the ability to raise finances. Norah bought the company herself on her own without a management team. Since then, she has been investing in a whole range of other businesses, so it was definitely a moment in time when her life changed.

Norah regrets not finishing her PhD. However, aside from that, she is happy with where she is at this time in her life. She declares that her eclectic career path has created the individual she is today and, on this journey, nursing helped to define who she is.

Norah believes it is important to contribute to society and to your local community. She believes it does not require a grand gesture; sometimes, it is about giving of one's time. She gets a lot of joy out of volunteer work; she sits on many charitable boards, and it is a philosophy that pervades the whole of her company. As a business, her company contributes, particularly to women's and children's charities. Norah says that she would not like to be on her deathbed answering her grandchild's question, "What did you do, Granny?" with, "I made a fast buck and turned companies around". Rather, she would like to think that she had made a bigger contribution.

COMPETENCIES, STRENGTHS AND VALUES

The ability to learn is a strength, and Norah was a constant learner. She did her postgraduate work in journalism and subsequently studied video production and direction. She studied strategic management and advanced strategic management over a course of a number of years. On the leadership side, she studied leadership and even delivered one of the Dame Kathleen Raven Collection of leadership lectures, which was a very prestigious honour.

The ability to take a risk is important. However, Norah cautions that it is important to balance the risk with good quality homework. She absolutely believes in the thoroughness of investigation, doing the market research, understanding everything about what one needs to know about the business, the ability to forecast, and consider the competition. Norah is always prepared to take the step towards the unknown and she also believes as time goes on that her intuition is much stronger. But she would always marry her intuition with the hard figures and the hard facts.

Norah recalls what a chairman of one of the boards she was on used to say: "If you fail, admit it, own up and move on". Norah notes that one of the things that defined her in the early years of growth was much more her failures than her successes. She learned far more from things that she did wrong than things that she got right just by chance. Norah learned early on that, if she had taken the wrong decision, the best thing to do was to quickly own up and move on.

Norah believes in being true to one's convictions. She finds herself naturally drawn to people who she feels have the courage of their convictions.

Norah says that success comes with a lot of personal sacrifice and missed family opportunities. In her role as a potential investor in another person's business proposition, she has to be sure that, going forward, they have the same personal ambitions as she has and the willingness to work hard.

CHARACTERISTICS OF LEADERS

As a leader, the individual needs to believe in themselves; not be afraid to take unpopular decisions; believe in what they are doing; and act exactly as you would expect them to do as they are role models. A leader needs to have a vision; be able to articulate a future, a plan, a better way, a better life, a mission; be able to share that vision; and be able to make the vision tangible to others.

Good leaders are very respectful of others, they actually try and achieve the vision tangibly. They are good role models because they always stick up for what they believe in and they never veer from it. They have a wider belief in relation to society and where they want to see their business positioned in terms of its community and social responsibility.

SIGNIFICANT CHALLENGES

Time was an enormous challenge for Norah as she continuously updated herself, sought to run a very big ambitious company, and have a personal life. This was because of her absolute fundamental belief that learning was not something she was ever willing to sacrifice. For Norah, the challenge always was staying abreast of the learning and the worldwide developments in her many businesses.

OPPORTUNITIES THAT ENHANCED SUCCESS / OBSTACLES ENCOUNTERED AND LESSONS LEARNED

Norah had a number of mentors on her professional journeys, including: Trevor Clay, Dame Kathleen Raven, Robert Tiffney and Anya Fossett Hennessy. Anya headed up the primary care division of the RCN and worked with the World Health Organization as its Chief Nursing Officer. Norah had many other people who provided mentoring roles for her at various junctures in her career and notes that at different times in one's life one needs different types of people.

Norah hates mission statements on walls. Everybody in the business needs to know what the business is about, the vision for the future of the business. If one was to ask anyone in her business from the receptionist through to the art director, they all would tell you exactly what the business is trying to achieve. Almost every month, there is some time away from the desk, where the team brainstorm different areas, so that everybody in the business understands where they are trying to go. Initially, the focus is on the big strategic setting. Then this is broken down into how everybody in the business is going to contribute, thus making the business plan tangible for all. People also need space and the flexibility to feel that they have control over their own environment.

ADVICE TO ASPIRING LEADERS

Norah feels that leaders need to have a well-researched vision or plan that they can articulate, share and implement.

Risk-taking is a must, yet it is only with maturity in terms of career progression that one can feel completely comfortable marrying intuition with the harder, more scientific, evidence, making sure that the two are balanced.

Lifelong learning also is very important.

Norah believes that, to be a leader, "you should be yourself but whatever feelings you may have – you should rely enormously on them and build on them".

CHAPTER 8
SISTER CONSILIO FITZGERALD

Brendan Noonan

Choose your team carefully and focus on positive people;
any negativity can destroy a team.

Sister Consilio is the founder and Chief Executive Officer of Cuan Mhuire, Farnanes, Co. Cork, Ireland's largest detoxification and rehabilitation service provider for those who are substance abusers.

She was born in 1937 in Co. Kerry. She trained as a general nurse and midwife in Cork and joined the congregation of the Sisters of Mercy in Athy, Co. Kildare, in 1959. It was while working as a

Sister of Mercy at St. Vincent's Hospital, Athy in the early 1960s that Sister Consilio witnessed the impact of alcohol addiction. Based on this experience, she founded Cuan Mhuire in 1966.

Today, Cuan Mhuire has communities in Dublin, Kildare, Cork, Limerick, Tipperary, Galway, Monaghan and Down. The total number of service users of Cuan Mhuire in 2009 was 3,000. It is a voluntary body and charitable trust and remains largely dependent upon voluntary support. Sister Consilio's work and the Cuan Mhuire model for dealing with addictions to gambling, alcohol and narcotics have been highlighted in several radio and television documentaries.

Sister Consilio is an Honorary Fellow of the Faculty of Nursing & Midwifery at the Royal College of Surgeons in Ireland and the Waterford Institute of Technology. She has won numerous awards through her work including, in 2010, an International Health Quality Award, the first time this award has been given to a rehabilitation service.

EARLY INFLUENCES

The main influences in Sister Consilio's life were her family and parents. Sister Consilio grew up in a home where her parents said little, but their *lived* example told all the family what they needed to know. The little that her parents did say was heard but what they did not say you said to yourself. An example of this was when she was going out dancing in her teens, she always waited for her mother to say something like "Mind yourself", or "Be good", but her mother never said it. This encouraged Sister Consilio to say it to herself. Her parents were hard workers, set a good example, built trust and gave the children the experience of being loved. These were very great graces for a child to receive.

Her parents never asked anyone to do something they would not do themselves. They were always willing to go the extra mile without being asked. For the first year of each of her children's lives, Sister Consilio's mother slept with the child in her arms because she did not trust the child in a cot. Sister Consilio believes that she got enough love in that first year to do her for the rest of her life. This love gave her a comfortable and secure feeling. She says the love given from our parents keeps us from having to go looking for it or for very poor substitutes for love.

Her mother's Christian faith also was influential, as was the support of neighbours who were an extension of home and respected and valued as important.

In nurse training, teamwork and its importance influenced her. In her religious life, the Reverend Mother of the Mercy Convent in Athy, where Cuan Mhuire began, had an influence on her. At that time, Cuan Mhuire would not have fit in with the way of life in the convent or what was expected of nuns. But Reverend Mother was the kind of woman who, if she thought you were doing something for someone else without thinking about yourself, she would not stop you. That was an important influence on how matters developed. Because of the Reverend Mother's trust, Sister Consilio felt compelled to be careful with her activities and to consider her leader at all times. One night, when travelling in a speeding car to visit someone in hospital, the thought in the front of Sister Consilio's mind was not about injury to herself but about how difficult it would be for her Reverend Mother if she had an accident.

Sister Consilio thinks trust is integral to life and one has to nurture it. This can be very hard at times. For example, in a house where you have individuals recovering from addictions, you have to draw a distinction between the person with whom you build up trust, and the addictions themselves, which can never be trusted. You have to be so vigilant in order to be safe.

Sister Consilio's mother would *always* say, "Like a good girl would you ever ..." and so she grew up believing everyone was good, including herself. This is a priceless gift for parents to give to a child – and it cost nothing at all! Every person who arrives now at Cuan Mhuire is missing the fact that they are good and it is the role of the staff to instil this message.

Another influence was Bishop Kavanagh, who was trustful, listened and was truly attentive to her aspirations. Also, family members offered unconditional support.

MAJOR LIFE EVENTS

Sister Consilio constantly stated that her mother was the person who made her who she is today.

Also, the residents treated in Cuan Mhuire have been a major source of life events. They have helped her to be aware of the need to keep changing – and to be open to change. In interacting with residents, she can see her own shortcomings. The privilege of being with them and being there for them continues to challenge her at all times. When they come to the service, many are at a very low ebb, often out of touch with reality, and quite ill. They may have unrealistic expectations. Many do not want to change, or do not understand the need for change in themselves. Working with individuals with addictions can be very demanding. The manipulation of addiction itself tests and tries you. Nevertheless, the programme is about life and living and one has to see beyond behaviour in order to see the beauty, goodness and the giftedness of the person.

In the early days of Cuan Mhuire, Sister Consilio perceived herself as a nice, gentle, little lady, trying to look after people, running downtown if someone was in bad shape, helping to get a number of people sober – and then three or four of them might fall around the floor drunk and abusive. This was as well as doing her work at the convent, where she often got into trouble for missing religious community events such as prayer time. She would get angry at the situation and speak about her responsibilities to the residents but, over time, realised that the ethos came from herself and she wanted to help – that was the way she was.

VISION FOR YOUR LIFE'S WORK

Sister Consilio believes that God has a plan for every person, which is a freedom and relief for her, because then she does not have a plan for herself or for Cuan Mhuire. She takes every day as it comes and lives in the *now*. She feels that satisfaction with life is received by following the plan that God has made, which is the only way to real happiness. There were indeed times that she was asked to do something that was part of God's plan, but she might not have fully realised it at the time. For example, she joined the Sisters of Mercy in Athy and, after profession, worked in the hospital in Athy for three years. Then her Mother Superior asked her to work in the convent kitchen, which she did as she felt it was part of God's plan. She feels that, if she had not done as asked (and stayed in the hospital instead), the State would never have ended up with the Cuan Mhuires that we have in the country today; Cuan Mhuire would have developed within the hospital services and she and the service would have stayed there.

At the moment, there is a lot of work to be done for young people who have addiction problems. Sister Consilio's vision is to recruit and retain committed vocation-driven people to work with these young people. Her vision for service is based on a philosophy that no two people are the same, thus each has to be treated differently based on their needs. She attributed learning this basic tenet from her father who, one day when feeding cows, was giving different food to each animal. When questioned, he explained that each cow was different: one giving milk all winter; another being bigger than others in the herd; another due to deliver a calf shortly. Her father therefore taught her to treat all people and situations on their own merits. Thus she understands that no two people in Cuan Mhuire have the same needs or backgrounds. Sister Consilio contends that, if you treat people with addictions or staff in the same manner, then you are doing a great disservice. Everybody has to be seen as the individuals they are.

COMPETENCIES, STRENGTHS AND VALUES

Resilience is a strength and competency. Sister Consilio also sees herself as loyal and faithful to whatever she takes on. She thinks *staying with something* no matter what and recognising that there always will be detours is important.

Being there for people is also a strength and she tries to spend as much time as possible with people.

She attests to the fact that she has many weaknesses, including being addicted to trying to change people whom she realises eventually changed her. A further strength comes from her Christian faith and her trust in this faith.

CHARACTERISTICS OF LEADERS

Humility, good example, hard work, commitment and dedication, putting others first, being loyal and silent are characteristics required of leaders. Listening, being respectful, not wasting energy on irreverent issues and moving on and parking what happened in the past also are important.

Leaders need the ability to identify the strengths of the people they work with and, in so far as is possible, to give them an opportunity to use these strengths: let people grow and continue to affirm them.

SIGNIFICANT CHALLENGES

Sister Consilio thinks that every day is a challenge when dealing with human beings, particularly those with addictions.

She identified other challenges as raising the money for the service (for wages, food and for the upkeep of the facilities and for staff who are so professional and committed to their work) and keeping the Government's respect. Treating all vocationally-driven voluntary bodies fairly in the provision of funding is a significant challenge.

Working towards accreditation was a great, and very rewarding, challenge. It was a wonderful experience working with a great team of experts; each person rose to the challenge.

ADVICE TO ASPIRING LEADERS

Sister Consilio's advice is to have humility, understanding and gentleness; be an easy person to talk to; listen well; make time for people; and be non-judgemental. Be caring; see the person rather than the job. Keep your mind to yourself about the people with whom you are working.

Teamwork is important; having a team that is bubbling over to help you, just because they are part of the team, is a huge asset – they will feel important, they will feel loved; they will know that you have their interests at heart; they will live or die for you and for those that you both care for and serve. You need people on your team who see the stars all the time.

Leadership is humility with fierce resolve.

Find a prayer that will be meaningful to you, read it to yourself throughout the day. It is something to hold on to that will help you through the difficult times and will help you to thank God for all the good times, and for His plan for you, as it unfolds in your life, and in your calling as a nurse and a leader.

CHAPTER 9
DEIRDRE GILLANE

Teresa Wills

*Never give up and do not expect everybody to be as
enthusiastic and ambitious as you are.*

Deirdre Gillane until 2011 held the position of Special Advisor to
An Taoiseach Brian Cowen, Teachta Dála (TD), Head of the Irish
Government. She was involved in the implementation of
government policy and priorities from the *Programme for
Government.*

Born and raised in Cork, the eldest of five, Deirdre qualified as a Registered General Nurse in Cork Regional Hospital (now Cork University Hospital (CUH)) and worked there for 10 years as a nurse, before embarking on a successful career as an advisor in politics. She started working in the Department of Health & Children in November 2000 and was Policy Advisor to Micheál Martin TD when he was Minister for Health (2000 to 2004), Minister for Enterprise, Trade & Employment (2004 to 2008) and Minister for Foreign Affairs (2008 to 2010). Prior to this appointment, Deirdre was Industrial Relations Officer with the Irish Nurses Organisation (INO), covering Dublin and the former Midland Health Board and Mid-Western Health Board.

EARLY INFLUENCES

Many people influenced Deirdre along her interesting career pathway, including her family, school teachers, nursing tutors and work colleagues.

Her mother worked full-time for 44 years up to her retirement and raised five children at the same time. She was very influential in Deirdre's life and had a strong work ethic. School days in St. Angela's also had an influence. She attended an all girl's school, was appointed head girl at school and was very active in sports. Deirdre talks in a very positive manner about how she received a very broad education in the humanities and care roles in society, about making a contribution to society and carrying out one's civic duties.

Her nursing tutors who played a significant influential role were Eileen Kelly, Finola O'Sullivan and Geraldine McCarthy. These three academics were good leaders and she admired their enthusiasm and knowledge. They were very interested in the politics of nursing as well as the politics of the hospital. They would make you proud to be a nurse.

Sister Killian in the School of Nursing also was an influence as she was an excellent manager of the school and had the ability to look after people without even telling them.

Work colleagues such as Micheál Martin (TD), Gobnait O'Connell (political advisor) and Mary Power (industrial relations officer) influenced Deirdre; she describes them as articulate and professional. Gobnait was not only a good friend but a good influence in her life, as Gobnait was very political and passed on that interest to Deirdre. Micheál Martin and Deirdre worked together in the Department of Health & Children for over four years. Prior to entering politics, Micheál was a secondary school teacher and was in the Association of Secondary Teachers of Ireland, so they had similar backgrounds and shared a very strong work ethic. Since both were from Cork City, they also knew similar people as well as the issues that were important across the political spectrum in Cork.

MAJOR LIFE EVENTS

The health 'cut-backs' were introduced in Ireland in 1987, at the time of Deirdre's transition into the INO, the union that represents nurses and midwives in Ireland. She was then a student representative on the Executive Council of the INO. When salary decreases were introduced for students in Donegal in 1987, this issue activated her and other student nurses to attend union meetings and get involved. The experience got them active locally and subsequently they met and experienced the difficulties felt by nurses in general.

When she qualified in 1989, there were few posts available for registered nurses and many of her nursing colleagues went to England and the United States to work. Deirdre had applied to go to the US. However, she was approached by Lil Kelly, the Director of Nursing at the time and asked to cover sick leave on night duty. That is how she got a job in nursing in CUH. She was on temporary nights and, after a year and a half, she got a permanent job in the hospital. She worked in CUH for 10 years before embarking on a successful career in politics. Her original ambition was to stay at CUH and work her way up through the management structure. She worked in the capacity as acting junior ward sister before she left the hospital. The post for ward sister was advertised but, as you needed to be qualified for five years to apply, she was unable to apply for this position.

Deirdre always was interested in challenging herself and discovering what she was capable of doing. She was involved in the INO for six years, representing the views of student and staff nurses in the hospital. Subsequently, she was successful in securing a job as Industrial Relations Officer with the INO. She was located in the INO office in Limerick City (1996 to 1999) and at central office in Dublin (1999 to 2000). In 1999, the first national strike in nursing took place. Deirdre says that was not an enjoyable experience either for nurses or members of the public. Deirdre believes on a personal level that there should be a 'no strike' clause for nurses. Deirdre thinks that some people who were promoted in nursing were not necessarily leaders but got into positions of authority that hampers the profession at times. Management training and the degree programme in nursing has made an impact and continuing education is a must for nurses at all levels. People management skills are a pre-requisite for any management post but particularly nursing.

Her next position came about as a result of her very good friend, Gobnait O'Connell, being killed tragically in a car crash in 2000. Gobnait was the first nurse to be a political advisor in the Department of Health & Children. Minister Micheál Martin appointed Gobnait in February 2000, a month after he started working in the Department. Following the tragic loss of Gobnait, Micheál Martin asked Deirdre to become his policy advisor. She started working in the Department of Health & Children in November 2000 and continued to work with him for 10 years, including time in the Department of Enterprise, Trade &

Employment (four years) as well as the Department of Foreign Affairs (two years).

The transition from the Department of Health was a challenge, as the Department of Enterprise, Trade & Employment oversees the Labour Court and Labour Relations Commission, while the Department of Foreign Affairs deals with all foreign relations. Deirdre's industrial relations experience with the INO assisted her greatly in these positions.

Deirdre's career trajectory saw her become an advisor to An Taoiseach Brian Cowen TD from May 2010 until March 2011. Obviously, this was a very challenging period for the country, given the economic, financial and political difficulties encountered. It was a huge learning curve for her. However, her experience of working as a political advisor for the past 10 years helped her in this new role.

The most important thing she has learned in politics or in any department is to show and gain respect when interacting with people.

VISION FOR YOUR LIFE'S WORK

Deirdre's vision for her life work is to make a contribution no matter what she is doing.

COMPETENCIES, STRENGTHS AND VALUES

Deirdre's strengths are her motivation, values and work ethic. She acknowledges that she comes from a hardworking family and that she is a straight talker. She does not give an opinion on something that she does not understand and, if she does not understand something, she will ask about it. Other attributes include being honest, hardworking and having the ability to be analytical.

Deirdre is immensely proud of her career as a nurse and believes that nursing gives you a fantastic broad education and teaches you how to communicate. Deirdre says that another of her strengths is her ability to be a good listener. Nursing teaches you this and Deirdre feels no matter where she works she can survive because she has learned the skill of communication.

CHARACTERISTICS OF LEADERS

Deirdre describes leaders as being open, approachable and motivated.

She believes that the best way to nurture people is through having respect and trust and being able to articulate what you want out of the team and maintaining standards.

SIGNIFICANT CHALLENGES

The loss of a significant friend, Gobnait O'Connell, was a major challenge for Deirdre and changed her whole career.

Deirdre describes her role as Policy Advisor in the Department of Health & Children as being very challenging but enjoyable. Her knowledge of the health service enabled the Minister to get advice from someone who had worked at the coalface, rather than a civil servant who had no healthcare delivery experience. Deirdre would advise on how policy decisions would translate into making the health service a better place for patients and staff. The introduction of the nursing degree in 2002 was a particular case in point. Replacing student nurses with a ratio of qualified staff and non-nursing staff was as a result of numerous discussions. Full implementation of the Commission on Nursing's recommended actions also took a lot of time. Working on the smoking ban was another highlight, as Ireland was the first country to introduce a nationwide ban.

Other challenges included working on the Health Strategy in 2001, which outlined health policy for the next 10 years. The *Acute Hospital Configuration Report*, known as the '*Hanly Report*', also was challenging. This report outlined the reasoning for centres of excellence and ensuring patients would be seen by the right people in the right centre at the right time, thus maximising survival rates. There was a huge political backlash but Minister Martin remained determined to do the right thing. This remains health policy today and has been implemented in the cancer area. It will take another few years to implement it in other services but it was significant for Deirdre to be there at the start.

Most of the difficulties Deirdre encountered when she was an advisor in the Department of Health & Children were related to the entrenched beliefs of different professionals who worked together in healthcare but looked at their own profession and working conditions in isolation. The impact on the health service in general and the patient would be mentioned last in their discussions. Another challenge was dealing with the press, as their understanding of nursing, nurses or the health service was often superficial.

OBSTACLES ENCOUNTERED AND LESSONS LEARNED

Deirdre gets annoyed and frustrated when there is no learning from mistakes that were already made. For example, trying to get a legitimate point across where people will not listen because the emotive side of an argument gets precedence.

The nursing strike in 1999 was not a good experience. There should have been an alternative approach rather than an all-out dispute. Even though staff did work in urgent areas without pay, Deirdre believes that the 1999 nurses' strike damaged the respect and credibility that the nursing profession always had with their focus on placing the patient first. Over the last 10 years, the Irish Nurses and Midwives Organisation (previously the INO) has become very political and that is the vast majority of exposure the public get to nursing now. She thinks it is very unfortunate that you rarely see programmes about public health nurses or midwives or general nurses caring for people. She also thinks that the only time the public hear about nurses and midwives is when the union representatives are on the media talking about pay cuts, industrial disputes or patients on 'trolleys' in Emergency Rooms.

ADVICE TO ASPIRING LEADERS

Deirdre's advice would be to never give up and do not expect everybody to be as enthusiastic and ambitious as you are in relation to nursing. Whilst Deirdre acknowledges that the education of nurses has undergone rapid and progressive change over the past 10 years, she advises that nurses need to be more politically aware.

She comments that the key to moving forward to meet the needs associated with a changing healthcare environment is to value the importance of education. Deirdre is immensely proud of her career as a nurse and would highly recommend it as a fantastic career choice as it gives you wonderful opportunity to care for people and travel the world.

Deirdre concludes with the following statement: "I love nursing, I never regret my 10 years in nursing practice and it would be the best part of my career so far ... obviously the last 10 years have been extremely interesting, and fascinating, but my nursing is always very special to me ...".

CHAPTER 10
EILÍSH HARDIMAN

Nuala Walshe

*Know your core business but trust your instincts and
consider your gut reactions.*

Eilísh Hardiman is Chief Executive Officer (CEO) of Tallaght
Hospital, Dublin, since August 2011. Prior to this, she was CEO of
the National Paediatric Hospital Development Board (NPHDB), a
pivotal position in the largest capital project in healthcare in
Ireland, with the specific purpose of planning, designing, building,

furnishing and equipping of the new national children's hospital, involving relevant parties, including the three children's hospitals.

Eilísh completed her nurse training in Sligo, qualifying as a registered nurse in 1986. She completed a BSc in Nursing at the University of Ulster, Coleraine, a Postgraduate Diploma at the University of Ulster, Jordanstown and an Executive Master's in Business Administration (MBA) at the Smurfit School of Business in 2007. Like many of the students attending the Smurfit School, she completed the MBA while at the same time juggling the demands of a senior management position and of family life, which at the time included one year old twins.

Eilísh worked for 19 years in St. James's Hospital, Dublin, progressing from Staff Nurse to Director of Nursing within her first 10 years there. In 2005, she was appointed as Deputy CEO / Operations Manager in the hospital, her first senior appointment outside of the nursing profession and the beginning of her general management career. St. James's Hospital is a large academic teaching hospital, has over 4,500 staff and strong links to Trinity College Dublin. Three years later, she was appointed to her position as CEO within the NPHDB. In late 2011, she was appointed to the position of Chief Executive at Tallaght Hospital.

EARLY INFLUENCES

Eilísh comes from an agricultural background. She is the eldest of five children and growing up in a farming environment as the eldest child had a significant influence on her values and work ethic and ultimate success.

After completing secondary school, she briefly enrolled in a laboratory sciences course but quickly realised she preferred working in a more frontline profession. She applied for and was accepted to study nursing in Sligo General Hospital. There were only 15 others in the class and they were fortunate to experience an extremely personalised and patient-centred approach to nursing education. Her nurse tutor, Mr Jim Callaghan, was definitely one of the people who influenced her in her early career.

Jim used to encourage Eilísh to do things a little bit differently. For example, during her first clinical placement, she came across an approach by nurses to the management of a patient's horrendous pressure ulcer using egg whites, oxygen and insulin. She was fascinated by this and, with her typical enthusiasm, went to the school library during her split shift to read about it. She ended up talking to Jim about research, wound management and evidence of outcomes in clinical practice. He told her very simply to get the facts – this was a very key message. She spent the two hours of her split shift break reading about wound management and found that there was no basis for the egg white, oxygen and insulin treatment. Jim sent her (as a preliminary student) back to the ward to talk to the staff nurses and the ward sister and to show them the wound management evidence based on research. They listened and stopped the practice and adopted treatments underpinned by evidence. Thus she learned early on that a key way to change things is to produce the evidence.

MAJOR LIFE EVENTS

Eilísh qualified as a nurse in 1986. Most of her classmates applied to undertake specialist postgraduate nursing courses but Eilísh opted to undertake a nursing degree course at the University of Ulster, Coleraine. She spent summers working in the USA and Christmas and Easters working as an agency nurse in London to pay her university fees and associated costs. Attending university was a major life event; it opened her eyes to the science and art of nursing, how to write academically, how to collect and analyse data.

She returned to Dublin in 1990 and worked as an agency nurse in all of the Dublin academic teaching hospitals. Her objective was to explore which of these hospitals she would best fit into and would allow her to develop. She opted for St. James's Hospital and started in the Emergency Department for about 18 months before undertaking a post-graduate diploma course in gerontological nursing. Subsequently, she worked in the long-term care environment and in a rehabilitation ward at St. James's Hospital, where she became a ward sister.

During her years at St James's Hospital, she became involved with the Irish Nurses Research Interest Group (INRIG) and was quickly exposed to Ireland's nurse leaders (Brigid Tierney, Judith Chavase, Pearl Tracey, Peta Taaffe, Margaret McCambridge and Maeve Dwyer), as she was keen to be involved in nursing research. They included her in INRIG and she became its secretary; this gave her the opportunity to meet and converse with nurse leaders from whom she learned a great deal.

Because she was involved with the Irish Nurses Organisation (INO), the first nurses' strike had a significant impact on her career development and gave her exposure to the leadership challenges experienced by the profession at the time. When the Commission on Nursing was established (1997), she was given the opportunity to represent frontline nurses on the Commission, which provided a remarkable opportunity to meet and work with extremely talented and well-informed people. It also meant that, at a relatively early stage of her nursing management career, she was exposed to the wider healthcare system workings and issues.

Rosemary Ryan, Director of Nursing, John O'Brien, Chief Executive Officer, Professor J.B. Walshe and Professor Davis Coakley, all of whom worked in St. James's Hospital, influenced Eilísh at different times of her nursing management career, as organisational structures and care management processes changed at St. James's Hospital.

VISION FOR YOUR LIFE'S WORK

Her vision at the time of the interview was focused on the new hospital – that is, planning, designing and building a children's hospital that is as good as the best in the world. More importantly, the vision relates to how the service will be delivered and managed with safe and expert care of children the utmost priority. It is not just about the building, which of course will improve fundamentally the outcomes and patients' and families' experiences compared with current conditions where every night hundreds of parents are sleeping on mattresses on floors.

COMPETENCIES, STRENGTHS AND VALUES

Competencies include a willingness to stand by one's beliefs, high quality care, equitable access and evidence-based decisions; and to take advantage of opportunities as presented and move outside one's comfort zone and take some calculated risks.

CHARACTERISTICS OF LEADERS

A good leader will have a clear vision and realistic goals and be able to articulate them clearly and communicate them effectively. She/he must also be prepared to do what is ethically and morally correct and be prepared to accept the consequences of decisions taken.

Good leaders know their core business and seek advice from experts, where appropriate. They are prepared to mentor and support those who need development. They are prepared to work as hard as every member of the team and earn rather than demand the respect of colleagues and those who report to them.

SIGNIFICANT CHALLENGES

Eilísh was secretary of the strike committee in St. James's Hospital during the first national nurses' strike in 1999. Those nine days were some of the hardest and most stressful days of her career to date. The strike was a life-changing event, as she was suddenly strike secretary, catapulted into a position of responsibility for care and services across the whole hospital. Eilísh and two colleagues had responsibility for the hospital during those nine days. Her overwhelming concern, which was successfully addressed, was to prevent patients from harm and, at the same time, to ensure that working relationships across professions were not damaged.

Working as Nurse Practice Development Co-ordinator at St. James's Hospital was challenging for different reasons. These were challenging times as it was predominantly her peers (Assistant Directors of Nursing) that Eilísh was dealing with and change was not easy for some. She slowly and directly worked to bring people on board with the goal of improving practice.

As Director of Nursing (a post to which she was appointed at 36), she had many obstacles to overcome and, during the five years in post, encountered many challenges. She was committed to the Clinical Directorate structure and, over the years, built up a strong team of Directorate Nurse Managers, reporting to a Clinical Director for Nursing Services in the Directorate. Her colleagues initially were somewhat apprehensive about the clinical directorate structure as they were concerned that the Director of Nursing did not have direct control over nurses. She argued then, and still believes, that devolved decision-making, responsibility and accountability for service must be supported at Directorate level and, in her case in St. James's Hospital, no one person can directly manage up to 1,650 nurses. She viewed herself as the corporate and professional head of nursing. She communicated very clearly that she expected the same standard of care and opportunities for professional development across the clinical directorates. But operationally, the clinical directorate team worked as a unit appropriate to their service. She gave the nurse managers the autonomy to do things differently and encouraged them to share and learn from each other. As Director, Eilísh took on broader corporate responsibilities. As Deputy CEO / Director of Operations for three years, Eilísh was accountable for the 24-hour operation of the hospital. This demanding and challenging post meant that she had to work with and through the wider workforce to effect change, service development and quality care at St. James's Hospital.

Eilísh's post as CEO of the National Paediatric Hospital Development Board held challenges of a different nature and scale. The Board had statutory responsibility and reports to the Minister. Its statutory remit is to plan, design, build, furnish and equip the new children's hospital (a €650 million capital project). This is a highly complex and political project that has attracted public and media attention. It involved exposure to and direct contact with officials in the Health Service Executive, the three children's hospitals and the Department of Health.

OPPORTUNITIES THAT ENHANCED SUCCESS

The initial opportunity to complete a nursing degree, when it was not the norm, almost certainly enhanced her career. This gave Eilísh the skills, competencies and confidence to progress her professional career. Nineteen years in different posts (from staff nurse to Deputy CEO) in St. James's Hospital provided excellent opportunities to prove her management and leadership abilities.

While Director of Nursing, she was very involved at corporate level. She commissioned the hospital concourse and the underground car parking, and chaired the steering group responsible for the implementation of the enterprise resource planning system, which involved the procurement and implementation of financial control systems. She was very involved in achieving hospital quality assurance and accreditation and, in the absence of a Human Resource Manager, oversaw the human resource department for six months.

Progressing her educational development by undertaking an MBA seemed a logical step. Eilísh won *The Sunday Times'* scholarship to enter the Smurfit Business School. It offered a great opportunity to network with a wide group of managers, leaders and entrepreneurs. The majority of the other students came from the private sector, were in their late 20s, and were supported by their companies. While attending the course, Eilísh was in her late 30s, and with twins on maternity leave from the public sector. Although the differences were there, she met some fantastic people and learned a great deal from being exposed to their ideas and ways of working. Reflecting on attending the course, Eilísh states that she had to be totally organised and, with the support from her husband, balancing family, work and study was like a military operation. Completing the MBA, while being enormously challenging, significantly equipped her to function at a higher level within a corporate environment.

ADVICE TO ASPIRING LEADERS

Eilísh states that, the further up the ladder you go, the tougher it becomes and, sometimes, it can be a lonely place. Get a mentor; be prepared to listen to their advice, respect and learn from them. Have a close friend, other than your life partner, who you can talk to confidentially. Have a vision and communicate this to those around you. The ability to bounce back – to be resilient – is important. Be constantly aware of your interpersonal skills. Get your facts right. Finally, put the patient at the centre of all you do and believe that your profession can make a difference to Irish healthcare.

CHAPTER 11
ANGELA KERINS

Lynne Marsh

Take the passion and make it happen!

Angela Kerins is Chief Executive Officer (CEO) of the Rehab Group, a leading voluntary organisation delivering high quality person-centred services to people with disabilities, older people and others who are marginalised. She has responsibility for over 17 companies and 3,500 staff.

Angela was born in Waterford and studied for a general nursing and midwifery qualification in the United Kingdom. After qualifying, she worked in the United Arab Emirates (UAE), Saudi Arabia and the USA and returned to Ireland in the mid-1980s.

In 1992, she began working with the Rehab Group as Director of Public Affairs & Care Services. In 1995, she was the founding Chief Executive of RehabCare, the health and social care division of the group, a post she held until 2006 when she succeeded to the role of CEO of the Rehab Group.

She has been Chairperson of the National Disability Authority since its establishment in 1999. In September 2007, she was appointed Chairperson of the Equality Authority. She is a member of several boards, including the Health Information & Quality Authority (HIQA). In 2003, she was awarded an honorary doctorate of Law (LD) by University College Dublin.

She has campaigned for worthy causes since she was young, and has been a driver for change, particularly in relation to disability, disability legislation and fair treatment for all.

EARLY INFLUENCES

Angela's father played a very influential role in her life and, from very early on, taught her about negotiation and flexibility.

She became interested and got involved in politics from an early age through her father, who was very involved in local and national politics. Thus, Angela developed an understanding of the political system in Ireland.

She had never planned to get extremely involved in politics but, during her early nursing career, her father was both surprised and shocked to see a photograph in *The Daily Telegraph* of his daughter, then a trainee nurse in England, campaigning for better pay for nurses. Angela always loved to campaign on behalf of causes she believed in, and was a wonderful campaigner for worthy causes.

MAJOR LIFE EVENTS

Angela did not practice nursing for very long. However, she did work as a staff nurse in intensive care for a period of time and felt that this gave her very good skills in communication, observation and report writing, which helped her enormously throughout her career.

She then made a decision to go to the UAE for a few years, which she thoroughly enjoyed. She subsequently worked with an American company in Saudi Arabia, specialising in rehabilitation. Around this time, her career moved into general management. Angela did not have a defined career plan, but knew she enjoyed management. She undertook a number of professional development courses, including financial management, to help her in her role.

In the mid-1980s, Angela returned to Ireland and began working in the Cheshire Home in a general management role. This proved to be a defining moment in her career, as it took her from her experience of institutionalised care in the hospital setting and gave her exposure to more person-centred, community-based care that provided a range of supportive accommodation, respite and community services for adults with physical disabilities. This position opened her eyes to the delivery of different models of care. Working for Cheshire Homes heightened her awareness and interest in disability issues and the struggle that people had to procure the supports needed to live their lives. This encouraged her to raise awareness of disability issues in the political arena.

She progressed to being Director of Public Affairs & Care Services in the Rehab Group, which was a training and employment organisation at that time. With the support of the then Chief Executive, she persuaded one local Health Board to provide funding for a community resource centre. This provided a new model of social care and independent living programmes for people with disabilities. The model proved successful and grew.

This organisation (RehabCare) now provides support to over 2,300 people annually, including specialist support services to adults and children with autism, services for people with Prader-Willi Syndrome and for people with an acquired brain injury, through resource centres, respite care, home care services, supported accommodation and residential services. RehabCare employs over 1,000 people.

Her progression to RehabCare was a significant learning curve and career move that challenged her thinking and helped her to develop more progressive models of care. It gave her an appreciation of the skills and abilities of people with disabilities and their contribution, both social and economic, to society. Angela believes that, whilst it is important that we provide people with necessary medical care, we need also to promote social care and independent living, as this is important in people's lives.

Angela has served on many State and voluntary Boards. She continued to campaign to raise awareness of issues affecting people with disabilities and their families, including advocating for improved legislation, recognition of rights and improvements in services and in regulations and standards for services. She was well-placed to negotiate with Government on public affairs, disability issues and disability legislation. By actively making political connections over her life across political parties, she has put herself in a position to challenge and change attitudes regarding people with disabilities.

VISION FOR YOUR LIFE'S WORK

Angela has worked very hard and has continuously ensured that her work performance attracted support. Certain opportunities have come about because of this drive. In 2006, she was appointed to the role of CEO of the Rehab Group, one of the largest voluntary organisations in Ireland, with significant operations in four European Union member states. She is only the third CEO in the organisation's 60-year history. Before the post became available, she began to focus on achieving the role, and she ensured she had an understanding and experience of all of the Group's diverse commercial and not-for-profit activities so that she was well-placed to attain the role.

She believes in teams and feels that it is best never to work alone, but to benefit from the experience, wisdom and ideas of a number of key and trusted people. When a job needs to be done, she has no difficulty in 'renting a crowd' to ensure that the best people to get the job done are available. Angela believes that having supportive individuals, who are personally well-known to you and can be trusted, is imperative to achieving goals. Confidence and the ability to be supportive of the team members are needed to achieve your life's work.

COMPETENCIES, STRENGTHS AND VALUES

Angela feels that her background as a nurse is an absolute strength. She feels that nurses are excellent multi-taskers and can support a multiplicity of issues around patients and families. They have excellent communication, observation and interpersonal skills.

What Angela also sees as a great trait in nurses is the ability to be direct and clear to the point, which is a trait that she sees in herself. She makes her point and the message is definitely clear. Additionally, Angela believes that as a nurse she is more than capable of seeing a project through to the end and that her nurse training helped her in this.

CHARACTERISTICS OF LEADERS

Angela believes that leaders are those who have the ability to stand up and be counted; lead from the front; be visible; build teams through support; and care for and drive people. They should have a desire to lead; be interested in processes; be a calculated risk-taker and be brave in doing so; be confident; give credit where it is deserved; openly and publicly reward others and say "Thank you"; acknowledge others for their contributions and influence in an organisation; and promote personal development programmes and staff training. Most importantly, though, do not be afraid to take informed risks.

SIGNIFICANT CHALLENGES

Managing a number of very different activities, and switching rapidly between them, requires you to be organised and to trust those around you to be effective in their roles. Business planning is essential, as you need to know where you are going, and how to measure success. However, you must also be flexible, and be able to adapt quickly. If an opportunity arises with a very short timeframe for it to be accomplished or acted on, then you must be able to work 'lastminute.com' but still manage to get the job done effectively.

OPPORTUNITIES THAT ENHANCED SUCCESS

Angela's nursing background definitely helped her succeed. She had the ability to move around and move forward. She firmly believes that you have to make yourself known and not be reticent about volunteering for responsibility. Angela is very openly and honestly ambitious and has achieved everything that she has achieved so far because of this ambition, drive and self-determination. If she wants something, she seeks an opportunity and works extremely hard to get it. This is usually in relation to a short-term goal but with the ability to broaden to a larger opportunity. Whether by luck or design, she has been able to seize opportunities that have been presented to her and she always ensures that she is genuinely interested in what she sets out to achieve.

Angela believes that opportunities are all around us and that we should pack a few opportunities in a backpack just in case! Not all opportunities will be realised immediately however, some will take longer to actualise. Lots of people do not see, or indeed seize, opportunities, so it is essential that they open their eyes to this potential. She also believes in "taking the passion and making it happen".

Additionally, Angela firmly believes that you cannot be successful alone. If you reward ambition, are ambitious for yourself and are focused, then you will take the organisation with you. Indeed, through encouraging ambition, the organisation benefits as it gets the best out of people.

OBSTACLES ENCOUNTERED AND LESSONS LEARNED

One major achievement in which Angela encountered obstacles along the way was the Disability Legislation Consultation Group. The diverse disability sector organisations of, and for, people with disabilities, families and service providers had not met together previously at all or had any real interaction. Many of the leaders of the organisations had never been in the same room, and they required significant support and encouragement to interact and to reach common ground. As Chairperson of the Disability Legislation Consultation Group, appointed by the Government, Angela sought to lead the group to recognise what it had in common and concentrate its efforts on achieving core principles. The group worked together to achieve the disability legislation, and what became later the National Disability Strategy.

Angela feels that, if you make a mistake, it is very important to pick yourself up and learn from the experience. She learns from any mistakes and ensures that the next time she has supportive processes in place.

Additionally, it is important to network where you can as a springboard for opportunities. Indeed, nurses, if in the right position, can influence positive change.

She also advocates that people are straight and respond best to honesty and forthright presentation. If she believes in a cause, she will fight for it. She will go the distance to change behaviour and fight for you, but if she feels that it is not working, having done her best, she will tell you straight.

Most significantly though, Angela will not tolerate any degree of cruelty or unfair treatment of clients, their families or staff.

ADVICE TO ASPIRING LEADERS

Listening to other people's views is essential, even when you think that you have made up your own mind. Sometimes, people have an interesting view that you have not encountered before, or a different take on things, which can be extremely valuable.

She believes that you need to explain to a nurse that she/he has a multitude of amazing skills, specifically in relation to communication: reading the room and the people, their interactions and values. However, nurses do not always promote themselves enough and, whilst they are confident in their own area, they need to broaden their vision and see the world in a new light. They need to open their eyes and minds to their own possibilities.

Irish people are always good at rewarding ambition to get the best from people. However, if you fail at something as an Irish person, it is never forgotten; in other countries, it is a badge of honour on the way to success! Failure should not be perceived as negative, because at least you tried. If you do not try, you will never get there. There are too many people looking back instead of looking forward, hence we need to change our mindset and take risks.

CHAPTER 12
ALICE LEAHY

Mary Rose Day

Be political, lead and speak out.

Alice Leahy trained as a nurse in Dublin and is now Director of
TRUST, a non-political, non-denominational voluntary body that
she established in 1975 to provide medical and related services for
people who are homeless and marginalised. TRUST is located in
the basement of the Iveagh Hostel in the Liberties in Dublin's inner

city. The ethos and aim of TRUST is to serve people who are homeless, encourage their development, and give their lives the dignity that is their birthright.

As a writer, commentator, broadcaster and lecturer, Alice has striven to promote an understanding of the needs of the outsider in society and thus help combat social exclusion. She also plays an active role in making submissions to Government departments.

Alice was a member of the Irish Human Rights Commission and a Board Member of Oberstown Campus, appointed to both by the Government. She is a former Chairperson of the Sentence Review Group, precursor of the Parole Board.

Alice has received a number of awards, including an Honorary Doctorate from the Faculty of Nursing & Midwifery in the Royal College of Surgeons in Ireland and an Honorary Doctorate from University College Dublin. These awards are seen by Alice as recognition of the work of staff, trustees, volunteers and the people who use the service at TRUST.

EARLY INFLUENCES

Alice Leahy was the eldest of five children. Her father was steward of a 400-acre estate belonging to Major and Mrs. Olivia Hughes, in Fethard, Co. Tipperary. Three generations of Alice's family – her grandfather, father and brothers – have worked on the estate, even though it has changed ownership over time. Alice's family had a very close relationship with the Hughes family and they exerted a major influence on her earlier years and life course.

According to Alice, Mrs. Olivia Hughes was one of the greatest Irish women of the last century. She was a woman of vision and a pioneer in many fields and was an avid promoter of better conditions for women at home. She spent time in America at the invitation of the W.K. Kellogg Foundation and there she studied the work of the 4-H Club program (rural youth clubs to support better agricultural education). In 1926, she established a branch of United Irish Women in Fethard (now known as the Irish Countrywomen's

Association (ICA)) and was a founder member of Country Markets with Muriel Gahan in 1947. She edited and published the ICA's first publication, *An Leabhair Féin*. Mrs. Hughes also was influential in the setting up of a Jubilee Nursing Service in Fethard. Alice recounted that, up until her death, she maintained an interest in Alice's work, writing to her and always anxious to meet her during visits home and she was always very encouraging.

Major and Mrs. Olivia Hughes and Alice's family were instrumental in giving Alice many opportunities to develop and grow her life skills and vision. Growing up in this environment gave her a strong sense of community values and beliefs. Alice worked on the estate during holiday time from an early age, picking fruit, feeding animals and caring for the environment. Mrs. Hughes, Alice and others set up a junior branch of Macra na Tuaithe in her home and there she became involved in public speaking, debating, drama and project work.

Major Hughes gave Alice six guinea pigs to support one of her research projects (in Macra na Tuaithe). He put her in touch with a laboratory at Trinity College Dublin (TCD) and the guinea pigs were used as part of a research project. Every few weeks Alice put the guinea pigs into boxes and cycled three miles to put them on the train to Dublin. A telegram to TCD ensured that they were met at the train station. Alice was runner-up in the *Young Farmers of the Year Award* in South Tipperary, for the planning, management and budgeting of the project. She attended the ICA's An Grianán centre for a number of weeks on scholarship and was involved in courses in art and crafts, cookery, leisure, personal development and public speaking. Growing up, she read the daily newspaper, the UK *Farmer's Weekly* and the *National Geographic*. This helped her become more aware of global and local issues.

Alice's family were influential in her growth and development. Her father and grandfather both received medals from the Royal Dublin Society for 50 years' unbroken service in agriculture. Her mother, Mrs. Hannie Leahy (née Crean), now in her 90s, was a major influence in her life. She is the remaining founding member of the first branch of Country Markets. Both parents were skilled in caring, budgeting, account-keeping and management, together with conservation, recycling and waste management before the term was coined. Alice's mother continues to write letters to the newspapers, particularly on rural issues, and Alice also contributes regularly to international, national and local media on issues in relation to marginalised groups. The community she grew up in, especially her extended family, the Hughes, and friends, gave her a unique vision and ethos for life.

Other people who influenced Alice were her maternal grandmother, paternal grandfather and grandaunts. Aunt Jo trained as a nurse in Daisy Hill Hospital, Newry; she loved reading, made wonderful apple tarts and looked stunning in a photograph, so proud in her nurse's uniform.

A teacher (Mrs. Julie Ryan) was another influence in Alice's life. She taught the children to sit still and emphasised the need to take time to look at one's soul. This influenced Alice, who strongly believes in meditation and reflection and encourages others to do the same.

MAJOR LIFE EVENTS

Alice has worked for many years with people on the margins of Irish society and this would not have been possible without the support of people from many walks of life. Two nurses – a home sister and a district nurse – influenced her during her training. The home sister showed great affection and understanding of people and always made excuses for behaviour. The district midwife (Biddy Butler) worked in the Rotunda Hospital in a deprived area of the city. Biddy had presence, was motherly and, no matter what conditions of squalor and poverty people lived in, she had a rapport with mothers that inspired confidence. She was a professional and treated students with the same caring approach and support.

The person who influenced Alice most over the years and helped her has been Geraldine McAuliffe, a nurse and Deputy

Director in TRUST. She has been significant to maintaining the ethos of TRUST, encouraging Alice to continue believing that anything is possible yet quietly getting on with life.

Alice says her key role is influencing and inspiring those who cross her path. Her family and nurse training gave her the skills to do the work she does.

Alice recounted feelings of frustration at times during her years as a nurse, due to the hierarchical structures that ensured an individual nurse's viewpoints "were often ignored" – particularly student nurses' viewpoints. She feels that, even to the present day, people who take a stand, try to make a difference or change the *status quo*, risk being excluded and becoming outsiders.

A number of factors influenced the pathways she took in life. She developed an interest and got involved in voluntary work, joining Voluntary Services International, working in the Benburb Street area of Dublin city. With another nurse, she established a Women & Mothers Group, focusing on diet, cookery, budgeting and personal development.

VISION FOR YOUR LIFE'S WORK

To be political; lead; speak out; work with people; encourage; challenge injustice; and make the space she lives in a better place.

COMPETENCIES, STRENGTHS AND VALUES

Have respect for people; be confidential; have organisational ability; be caring; listen; know your colleagues and be aware of their skills; be flexible; become an advocate on behalf of people, particularly those who are vulnerable, and listen to their stories.

Nurses need to be political, make submissions and use the media. Maintain your energy; be able to see and use opportunities that arise and find support in the most unlikely places. See life outside the box and move beyond your comfort zone.

CHARACTERISTICS OF LEADERS

The important characteristics of leaders are to be visionary; questioning; reflective; positive; energetic; challenging; charismatic; inspiring; and to use opportunities to instil hope.

Listen, inspire, encourage and look at new ways of doing things. Work hard.

Alice says that being a leader is not easy, it can be very isolating but being aware of that fact helps.

SIGNIFICANT CHALLENGES

Over the years, Alice feels that politicians and people in positions of power were naïve enough to think that TRUST would not be needed in the long-term. This view was shared by Alice and her team in the earlier days and they thought they would cease their work one day as all would be solved. Over 35 years, TRUST has made a significant contribution to the lives of people who are homeless and raised their profile across communities internationally through their daily work. Many people from all walks in life have given support, both moral and financial, and this has contributed to TRUST's survival. Alice's belief is that the State should provide for those who are marginalised, bearing in mind our *Constitution*.

The growing diversity of the Irish population in recent years means that the people attending TRUST come from all over the world. Some people attending the centre can be very challenging and growing racism poses significant health and safety risks for staff and people attending services. TRUST has ceased its open door policy due to the changing environment. These challenges require a lot of negotiation and skills, supporting, debriefing and protecting service users and staff. Staff need space and time to share and talk about good and bad experiences. They need to be affirmed, complemented and supported and this is all part of how they operate at TRUST.

Alice's message is that homelessness is a life circumstance; it could happen to any of us. Professionally and personally, the challenge for her is to maintain her beliefs, to value hands on work and to give time to people and not to allow this to be diminished by ignorance and nonsense.

OPPORTUNITIES THAT ENHANCED SUCCESS

The environment she grew up in, the support of her family and the Hughes family gave her a great start in life. While working in the Royal City of Dublin Hospital, Baggot Street, she was sent to the London Hospital by the Medical Board to source information in order to establish the first Intensive Care Unit (ICU) of its type in Ireland. While there, she met Dame Cicely Saunders, who was founder of the modern hospice movement, and was influenced by the multifaceted team approaches to care-giving and the involvement of staff at all levels. In 1971, Alice was Sister of the first ICU unit of its type opened in Ireland.

Alice found overcrowding, conveyor-type systems, insufficient staff and lack of consultation with nurses very difficult. Her decision to move out of the hospital system and work with marginalised people caused much debate and concern amongst her colleagues. She joined the Simon Community organisation (for people in need) and lived and worked in a condemned building, using her nursing experience to good effect. She never regretted the decision to leave the formal health service.

OBSTACLES ENCOUNTERED AND LESSONS LEARNED

Obstacles include increasing bureaucracy; the rush to change people; lack of vision and understanding; and poor and inappropriate services. The difficulties encountered daily relate to drug abuse, racism and inappropriate behaviour. Regular meetings with staff and board members as well as structured processes, policy guidelines and rules are necessary to support and overcome these obstacles, while not forgetting time for humour and laughter.

Working with professionalism and keeping sight of values, supporting the team and being aware of shared humanity are all important. Alice says there are increasing numbers of inappropriately and untrained personnel working in her field now without supervision, many of whom have assumed a status of major importance (much of this is due to outsourcing of services away from State bodies). Agencies can be antagonistic towards each other and often the politics and power struggles can be hidden and ignored. Support comes from the most unlikely places, not from where you think it will.

Meditation, exercise and saying it as it is have been helpful to her in overcoming obstacles.

ADVICE TO ASPIRING LEADERS

Her key message is to have confidence in what you do and not to be afraid to speak out. Some examples of how she has tried to promote an understanding of social exclusion are publications such as a one-day training pack, *The Homeless Experience*; three books: *Not Just a Bed for the Night* (1998), co-authored with Anne Dempsey and published by Marino Press, *With Trust in Place – Writing from the Outside* (2003), published by Townhouse and, most recently, *Wasting Time with People?* (2008), published by Gill & Macmillan; and social documentaries and DVDs, including *A Fragile City*, *Building Trust in the Community* and, in 2010, the *Would You Believe?* Documentary, *Wasting Time with People?*, which can be seen on the website **www.trust-ireland.ie**. This website is updated regularly and includes articles and letters to the papers going back over the years. She also developed two very successful national competitions for second-level schools on the theme of the outsider.

CHAPTER 13
EMILY LOGAN

Helen Mulcahy

Balance ideals and common sense.

Emily Logan is Ombudsman for Children in Ireland; she was the first appointee to this post (2004). The role of the Office of Ombudsman for children is set out in the *Ombudsman for Children's Act, 2002* and is divided into three functions: communication and participation; research and policy; and complaints and investigation.

Emily trained as a Children's Nurse in Temple Street Hospital, Dublin and subsequently worked in London, at Guy's Hospital and Great Ormond Street Hospital. In 1997, she returned to Ireland and worked as Director of Nursing at Crumlin Children Hospital, Dublin (1997 to 2001) and as Director of Nursing at the Adelaide & Meath Hospital incorporating the National Children's Hospital, Tallaght, Dublin (2001 to 2003).

Her area of expertise is in children's rights and advocacy and child protection. In her role, Emily has been vocal and prolific on many issues relating to the welfare of children – for example, children in detention centres; children living in care; and children without families. She has been described in the media as courageous and fearless in taking on an investigation of the Health Service Executive (HSE) and the Department of Health in relation to child protection in the Catholic dioceses. She takes her functions very seriously and is not afraid to take on the institutions of the State to provide a voice for the rights of children. Emily is clearly committed to improving the health and welfare of children in Ireland.

EARLY INFLUENCES

Emily's status of being a middle child in a family of seven was an influence. In a large family, one learns to be part of a team. In Emily's family, there was a strong sense of everyone working to maintain the household. Emily's mother was very influential; she was, and still is, liberal in her thinking. Emily feels her own sense of justice and responsibility developed from her mother's influence. She remembers quite clearly getting into trouble in school when 11 years old and owning up straight away because she believed it was right to take responsibility.

Her mother was very open in communicating, as was her whole family. Family members talked about whatever was bothering them; none were shy and family members learned to speak up for themselves. Emily had an active, energetic, childhood, running the roads, playing and walking to school. Emily believes these interactions with family and school friends were important in developing social skills.

One teacher in particular in primary school was an influence as she created a safe environment for all children. Her kindness and fairness, natural justice and her ability to ensure that no child was isolated or excluded were exemplary.

The influence in terms of choosing children's nursing in part stems from her mother, who had a fear of blood, but with seven in the family there were always cuts and scrapes, some of them necessitating a trip to hospital for stitches. Emily says that once her brother was bitten by a dog and, while her mother was running for the neighbours, Emily was in the bathroom dealing in excitement with the blood and the bite.

MAJOR LIFE EVENTS

Emily was just 18 when she began to study nursing and, at times, found the experience overwhelming. There was a lot of social deprivation in the catchment area of the hospital and she was conscious of the poverty and economic difficulties encountered by families. Many children had no visitors or were admitted with non-accidental injuries. There was a culture of poor communication within families and poor hygiene, leading to infestation of head lice in the children.

The environment of the hospital also was very controlling. She can remember being on night duty for three months and asking the matron for a night off for her sister's wedding and being refused. There was also a ward sister who catered to the needs of private patients in a different way to those of public patients. While she enjoyed her training, some examples of injustice stood out.

Working in Great Ormond Street Children's Hospital was a major life event. A choice of where one wanted to work was available. While the clinical work for children's conditions was not that different between Ireland and the United Kingdom (UK), there were many more complex cases – for example, children with human immunodeficiency virus (HIV) and severe combined immunodeficiency (SCID) – being treated and there was a lot more money available. Princess Diana was patron of Great Ormond Street and wealthy benefactors tended to donate CAT (computerised axial tomography) scanners rather than boxes of Milk Tray chocolates.

The culture of hospital care in the UK was definitely a major influence. The first time Emily saw a child die in a hospital in Ireland, she cried and was told to leave the room whereas the families were known intimately and people laughed and cried together in Great Ormond Street. Emily was just 25 when she applied for a ward sister position in the renal unit, which turned out to be a brilliant career opportunity.

Great Ormond Street was quite an expensive healthcare organisation and was branded as providing a quality service. It was quite challenging to be calling patients 'consumers' but there was also a challenge and freshness to the endeavour. At 26, Emily was working with business managers, which required a different mindset. If a 3% budget cut was required, everyone sat around and all took responsibility for cutting the budget. Business managers listened to the nurses' ideas – for example, suggestions about cutting expensive routine diagnostics without compromising the quality of the service. She developed a great amount of clinical knowledge and nurses were actively encouraged to question and challenge.

Sally Nethercott, the Director of Nursing in Great Ormond Street, was a big influence. She was young and dynamic. She had a different style; she was charismatic and praised staff and encouraged managers to recruit people who were smarter than themselves. She had great pride and a good business head. She allowed people to shadow her and to see how she worked. She was able to communicate very effectively across disciplines. She could convince other people and get her message across without resorting to emotion. There was a huge value placed on nursing and the hierarchical structure was not as obvious as it was in Ireland and this really helped to improve Emily's confidence. Sally encouraged Emily to consider promotion, which she achieved in a post in middle management. This culminated in her being involved in action learning sets and participating in an audit of critical incidents in the previous 10 to 15 years.

While Emily was in Great Ormond Street, the post of Director of Nursing in Crumlin Children's Hospital in Dublin was advertised. Emily was recruited to the post, despite the concern of the board of management that she was just 32 years of age. This was a clear indication of the culture she wanted to change.

VISION FOR YOUR LIFE'S WORK

Emily's vision changed throughout her career. However, she is inspired always in doing what she can to encourage a cultural shift based on her value of human dignity. She believes in taking responsibility for one's actions and that the concept of deference to authority needs to be challenged.

She has a need to see nursing develop and stand up for itself. Emily came back to Ireland just before the nurses' strike and was disappointed to see the handover of power to the unions. She does not doubt that there are issues around terms and conditions that require union involvement but she believes that there are better ways of developing as a profession.

COMPETENCIES, STRENGTHS AND VALUES

Emily learned many transferable skills from nursing – for example, her experience of dealing with situations of crisis, including cardiac arrests, has served her well. She is well able to provide a realistic assessment of a situation.

Other competencies include being analytical; strong; determined and passionate; holding no deference to authority; pragmatic; and well able to balance ideals and commonsense. Believing in what you are doing is also important.

CHARACTERISTICS OF LEADERS

Leadership is about the ability to inspire and to create a sense of purpose for those who share *and* who do not share a common goal. The characteristics that are important are versatility, decisiveness, openness and willingness to learn.

It is important *not* to surround yourself with like-minded people. You need to have a willingness to develop political acumen.

It is very important to have humility. One could become blinded by a position or power. It is so important not to lose sight about what the position is about and never get complacent.

SIGNIFICANT CHALLENGES

Emily was not very confident when younger; this posed a challenge that was rectified over the course of her career. Supporting people in the grip of fear while facing illness challenges one professionally and helps you grow.

The culture changes encountered working in the UK and in Ireland were particularly challenging. The cost of living in another country when flights were very expensive, thus making it difficult to come home to family, also was challenging. Returning to Ireland where friends had moved on with their lives was socially challenging for a while.

Being misrepresented by the press is an ongoing challenge.

OPPORTUNITIES THAT ENHANCED SUCCESS

Working in Great Ormond Street Children's Hospital and in her current position as Ombudsman for Children in Ireland has provided opportunities. Most recently, there have been opportunities for international collaboration as Emily has been appointed as European chairperson on the Ombudsman for Children Network and as such has been exposed to the incredible talent in the European forum working for human rights for children. In this, she has learned a lot about international diplomacy. The network members meet once a year; listening to counterparts in Eastern Europe is like hearing about experiences in Ireland 20 years ago. A meeting with an all-male delegation from the Turkish Parliament, where the environment for children rights is very different, was enlightening where a system of human rights for children was difficult to explain.

Experiences in the political environment and exposure to politics across political parties has enhanced her learning, as the Office of Ombudsman can have no political affiliation. This is critical because different political parties can think very differently about children's rights. Emily was appointed by the President of Ireland; this confers not only respect but also ensures that responses to any queries are forthcoming.

OBSTACLES ENCOUNTERED AND LESSONS LEARNED

Emily has learned that things that can be perceived as obstacles are not necessarily so. She has a healthy attitude to obstacles. When she first became a nurse manager, she was fearful and naïve and thought consensus was the way to operate but realised fairly quickly what she needed to find were people to support her. Some of the mistakes she made were in relation to making radical changes too abruptly or giving autonomy too soon. This caused people to get upset and confused because they could not handle the situation.

Other valuable learning was derived from working with the unions on industrial relations issues and negotiating realistic expectations. Undertaking a Master's in Business Administration enhanced her learning about strategies, and financial and business systems.

Emily has learned to become more self-aware; to overcome lack of confidence; to communicate to all groups of all types; to develop versatility and bring people with her; and to make tough decisions.

ADVICE TO ASPIRING LEADERS

Develop your own philosophy, values and beliefs; take risks; make tough decisions; do not be afraid; develop a network of support; do not isolate yourself; use self-development techniques; be positive, allow yourself to be led and influenced by positive role models; remember that principles of management are all the same; enjoy your work; don't neglect your own identity; talk to the media; and don't give your power away.

CHAPTER 14
MARY McCARRON

John Linehan

Without a deep commitment and passion for a subject,
leading change can be difficult.

Mary McCarron is Dean of the Faculty of Health Sciences at Trinity College Dublin. An international expert in the field of intellectual disability and dementia, she has played lead roles in a number of areas, including specialist memory clinics and service re-design.

She has been at the forefront in extending palliative care to persons with advanced and terminal dementia and other non-malignancies such as chronic obstructive pulmonary disease (COPD). Her research and teaching activities reflect her interest in ageing and health and she is active in developing educational initiatives with a focus on ageing. She is principal investigator for the first-ever study on ageing in persons with intellectual disability. This study has the potential to compare the ageing process in people with intellectual disability with other groups. Her work is widely published.

Mary is a consultant and spokesperson on ageing-related issues for key organisations in Ireland. She is a Research Assistant Professor at the Centre for Excellence in Ageing Services at the University at Albany, New York, where she consults on intellectual disability and dementia grants funded by the US Administration on Ageing.

EARLY INFLUENCES

Mary's mother exerted an early influence on her life. She described her mother as a very energetic woman, who had a very positive outlook on life and enjoyed people. She believes that her mother influenced her own leadership style in terms of the vision and energy she brings to all activities in her life.

MAJOR LIFE EVENTS

Mary's nurse training in intellectual disability was a key influence in her career. She describes how 'sameness' was never a concept evident in caring for people with an intellectual disability. Her strong sense of accepting differences in people comes from this experience.

She always had a sense of challenging the *status quo,* as she never liked routine. She describes how, from an early stage in her nursing career, she was always reflecting on how things are and how they could change for the better.

The core concepts of nursing embedded in her during her nurse training were enablement, empowerment, advocacy, and holism. These are some of the core values Mary believes are inherent in being a good leader. These characteristics are related to her leadership style in terms of empowering others and allowing them control over the change process.

Eva Wall, former Dean of the Faculty of Nursing at the Royal College of Surgeons of Ireland (RCSI), was a true visionary and someone who exerted an influence on Mary. Ms. Wall led efforts to professionalise nursing and set high standards of education and clinical practice in a time when nursing was in an early stage of developing an educational and research agenda.

VISION FOR YOUR LIFE'S WORK

Mary's vision for her life's work is focused on developing an evidence base for the future care of people with disabilities who are ageing and on influencing the standard of care that people with disabilities will receive.

COMPETENCIES, STRENGTHS AND VALUES

Mary described her strengths as a leader as being visionary and having the ability to articulate that vision. This she sees as being a key characteristic of a good leader. As a leader, she believes one needs to dream about how a service might look as part of this vision.

She considers that she has very good communication skills and has a great ability to listen to others. This, she believes, is strengthened by her continuing contact with people with an intellectual disability and their families and is important in keeping her in touch with clinical practice.

She describes herself as a highly committed person, very energetic, and one who has a very good sense of humour. She is creative and looks for innovative solutions to problems.

Mary believes in doing things well. Whatever she has an interest in, she commits totally to it and put all her energies into it. She is slow to lead out on issues where she is not totally committed to the vision herself. Openmindedness and a propensity for flexible thinking have been critical to her interest in new approaches and in looking for new ways of doing things. She has always felt that leaders are more likely to be successful if they are not rigid in their beliefs and actions. She had a sense that she naturally attracts people who want to become involved in bringing about change and, when taking on a leadership role, she tries to surround herself with like-minded people. Positive thinking and motivation in the face of adversity are important traits for any leader and Mary surrounds herself with positive people. She finds negative energy exhausting, consuming and destructive.

CHARACTERISTICS OF LEADERS

Leaders strive for excellence, while at the same time recognising that excellence is not static. She stated that leadership is about having a vision of where an organisation should be and having a key understanding of how to operationalise that vision. A key characteristic is the ability of the leader to communicate the vision and process to others within the organisation.

From her experience, she acknowledged that leaders also need to give a lot of themselves and be highly motivated by what they are pursuing. The motivation is not about the status of a post or the money, but rather the passion and interest in the subject matter. Mary suggests that, without a deep commitment and passion for a subject, leading change can be difficult. In essence, it is about having a real and genuine interest in bringing about change.

Mary has a very strong sense that leaders do not own the process but facilitate others to bring about change. She believes that leaders need to be approachable, motivated and strongly believe in not being in control or owning the process but in empowering others. In her role as a leader, she always tries to facilitate others to do their particular job well by putting the necessary structures in place to achieve success.

Mary has experienced many nurses in leadership positions believing that they own or control patients, the work environment and staff. This, she believes, leads to disempowerment of staff and less beneficial patient outcomes. She sees failure in leadership in terms of not empowering others and not allowing them to move forward. In Mary's opinion, interference by leaders not standing back to allow others to develop and taking too much control adversely affects the leadership role. Leaders must be perceptive in dealing with people, getting to know their staff and developing an ability to understand their strengths and weaknesses, knowing their moods and what makes them tick, and being able to handle any situation involving sensitive matters and emotional issues.

Leaders need to keep on learning, and to be able to recognise the need for, and adapt to, change quickly.

All leaders need to be prepared to do a lot of hard work but this has to be backed with a strong belief or conviction that it is worth doing. One needs to like what one is doing; if not, when times are tough or when negative people put obstacles in your way, you may find it difficult to realise the dream.

SIGNIFICANT CHALLENGES

Mary has met many obstacles in her leadership role. She feels that, in order to be a good leader, you must be persistent and have the courage to take risks, try something many times and in different ways before you get it right, and not to be downtrodden by the naysayers.

She tries to treat everyone the same, irrespective of who they are or where they are within an organisation. She does not believe in a hierarchical system and she states that that her leadership role is based on her three Fs: firm, fair and flexible.

Rapid changes in healthcare and technology are occurring and the change in the role of the consumer is a major challenge facing leaders within the nursing profession. Nurses need to recognise that knowledge does not rest with the nurse or lecturer but with the consumer, due to the ease of access to information. A key challenge is for nurses to recognise this and to continue to empower students and patients.

OPPORTUNITIES THAT ENHANCED YOUR SUCCESS

A wide range of opportunities in clinical practice, research and academia have enhanced her success. She also has created many opportunities for herself through her vision of where she believed she could contribute. She speaks of feeling privileged to have worked with so many wonderful people, in her clinical practice and in academia, and how they supported her in developing a set of skills that have helped her along her way.

Her energetic approach to life has meant that she has never stayed in one position for a long period of time. When she reaches a plateau, she moves along to fulfil her next vision or dream.

OBSTACLES ENCOUNTERED AND LESSONS LEARNED

Lessons have been learned from both good and bad experiences. The bad experiences were mostly around wrong decisions that meant the road to success was harder. Her theory about learning from mistakes is that, if you think you know best, then you need to realise that this may not always be the case.

Mary says that, when faced with people expressing negative views, you need to try to bring those people along with you, or make a decision to leave them behind, or accept the differences that exist and acknowledge that sometimes people are in a different place than you are.

She believes to be a successful leader one needs to try to get good people close to you, people that you trust, to bounce things off but who are not afraid to offer constructive criticism to you.

ADVICE TO ASPIRING LEADERS

Take opportunities to lead and do not be afraid; look at and learn from other fields outside of nursing; become political and develop connections and networks with external bodies.

A leader who learns about innovative models in healthcare through creating external networks then will be able to picture the world from a different place and anticipate what is required to meet the challenges ahead.

Nursing now is an expensive commodity but one that is highly valued by the public. The profession needs to focus more on outcome measures that clearly display the value, contribution and significant difference that nurses make to the lives of patients in their care.

Mary sees Irish culture as a significant hindrance in developing leadership in nursing. Irish people do not celebrate success and often do not see the value in what they achieve. Nursing should feature more in the media, such as on RTÉ's *Prime Time*, celebrating all that is good about nursing and midwifery in Ireland and articulating nurses' real contribution to healthcare in Ireland.

In Mary's experience, nursing has seen many recessions and the current one is no different. In the past, nursing has re-evaluated where it was and re-focused and set out a new vision for where it needed to go. Nursing in Ireland needs to do this again and it can do so with strong leadership.

CHAPTER 15
GERALDINE McCARTHY

Nicola Cornally

*Be confident in what you do; be ethical and respectful;
find learning in rejection; and find learning in things
that don't go your way.*

Geraldine McCarthy is Emeritus Professor at University College
Cork, concentrating on research. She was founding Professor of
Nursing and Dean/Head of the Catherine McAuley School of
Nursing & Midwifery, University College Cork (UCC) from 1994 to

2012. From 2010 to 2011, she also held the post of Acting Head of
the College of Medicine & Health at UCC, providing strategic
leadership in research and educational programmes in Medicine,
Dentistry, Therapies, Pharmacy, Nursing and Midwifery.

Prior to her appointment at UCC, she was Research &
Development Manager for Nursing at Beaumont Hospital, Dublin,
when three major acute hospitals were amalgamated to one new
site. She has held a number of other nursing positions in the United
Kingdom, United States and Canada.

She holds a MEd from Trinity College Dublin (TCD), and MSN
and PhD degrees in nursing from Case Western Reserve University
(CWRU), Cleveland, Ohio, USA.

She has been a member of a number of national and European
Union bodies, including the Commission on Nursing, The
Education Forum and the Task Force on undergraduate medical
education. Currently, she is a Ministerial nominee to the Health
Information & Quality Authority (HIQA) and to the Fulbright
Commission.

She has published and presented nationally and internationally.
Her research interests include chronic disease self-care and
management, especially among older persons. She leads the
Healthy Ageing Research Theme within the School and supervises
PhD, Professional Doctorate, and MSc Students. In addition, she is a
member of the local Health Service Reconfiguration Team that is
working to transform the Hospital & Community Health Services.

EARLY INFLUENCES

Key people who influenced Geraldine include her parents and
grandparents.

Her father played a significant role by instilling the value of
seeking and having a profession to sustain oneself throughout life.
Her mother complemented this by demonstrating a considerable
work ethic and was resourceful and resilient when faced with life's
challenges.

Connectedness with Irish culture was captured by her grandmother, a woman who grew up alongside Michael Collins. Stories of West Cork and Ireland's woe made Geraldine proud to be Irish and subsequently, despite leaving Ireland to work and study, she always returned. Her grandmother's influence extended well beyond this: it was during her grandmother's time of ill health that Geraldine, as a teenager, considered nursing rather than teaching. Her grandfather, a politician, broadened her awareness and interest in health and healthcare issues, due to his involvement in health services.

Early nursing influences included her first ward sister, a nun, who exemplified caring, Christianity and fairness, and her class mates, some of whom remain firm friends. Her nurse tutor spoke in a language that challenged her, yet Geraldine perceived this tutor to be a fountain of knowledge. Also influential were her supervisors in TCD, who guided her postgraduate work and gave constructive and positive feedback.

MAJOR LIFE EVENTS

The death of her father, and a short time after that, her grandmother and brother-in-law, left her with the feeling that one must have a balanced life. She felt that, in her primary and secondary education, she was continually compared to her older sisters and that her deficits, rather than her strengths, were always profiled. She admits to being timid during her school-going days but believed that negative experiences made her strong.

In nurse training, the patients she met and the friends she made were described as major life-changing events, as were the periods she spent studying at University College Dublin (UCD), TCD and CWRU. Indeed, working in America and Canada expanded her thinking, particularly in terms of the cultural experiences.

Other major life events included membership of various health and policy advisory groups. In addition, Geraldine organises an annual trip to Lourdes with nurses, doctors, students and patients from the Cloyne Diocese. This gives her the opportunity to meet people from the broader health service, while remaining in touch with current clinical practice.

VISION FOR YOUR LIFE'S WORK

While her grandmother gave her the vision and desire to have a career in nursing, it was her international nursing experience, where she encountered graduate nurses, that enhanced her vision for an all-graduate nursing profession in Ireland. She feels extremely lucky to have been able to see that come to pass in her lifetime.

Other aspirations included becoming highly experienced, skilled and educated to as high a level as possible. She continued to return to college and, after her nurse training, attended University College Cork (UCC) for a common science year before transferring to UCD to take the only university qualification available to nurses at the time (1977 to 1979): the Diploma in Nursing. Subsequently, TCD offered her a place on the Master's in Education degree, which was supported by a grant from 3M. She was a member of the Irish Nursing Organisation Executive at the time, which she believes put her in a position to see opportunities. She replied to an advertisement for a scholarship to study in the US for a PhD and successfully completed a Master's in Nursing degree and a PhD at CWRU, Cleveland, Ohio. On her return from America (1990), she was the first nurse in the country with a PhD in Nursing.

In her earlier years, academic opportunities for nurses were limited and spurred a vision to make a real difference. Her vision was clear: she wanted to seek and hold an influential position in education.

COMPETENCIES, STRENGTHS AND VALUES

Resilience and resourcefulness were described as key competencies that Geraldine holds. She ascribes these to her mother's philosophy. Also of importance is ethical stance in terms of doing the right thing and making sure everyone is treated in the same way.

One of her competencies is the ability to make decisions, based on factual information and reflection. Inextricably linked to this is the ability to live by the failure, if there is a failure, without taking any offence whatsoever and to move on.

Geraldine prides herself as being a good team-builder and values people for their ability but she cannot tolerate laziness or inefficiency. She describes herself as having a helicopter view, always looking at issues within the bigger picture.

In terms of values, the most important thing she feels is to value people and to try to understand the differences between them. She emphasises the need to find what people are good at. She values good, open communication, straight-talking and people who do not take offence or those who can move on and not be weighed down by something that happened in the past.

She also values hard work but stresses that family is imperative. The need for balance is evident and Geraldine stated that she does not like it when she sees people who do not detach from work.

She values very much the work that nurses do and commends them for staying in clinical practice.

CHARACTERISTICS OF LEADERS

According to Geraldine, to be a leader, you need to be fair; non-judgmental; a strategic thinker; bear no grudges; confidential; respectful; hardworking; knowledgeable; a team-builder; a risk-taker; and balanced.

SIGNIFICANT CHALLENGES

Leaving Ireland to study in the US was a significant challenge. Achieving an academic appointment in Ireland was a challenge because, up to the mid-1990s, there were no posts available. Preparing to compete for an academic position was difficult as there were no nurse academic mentors and nurses in clinical or administrative posts were not publishing their work.

In her early days at UCC, she was a woman in a man's world; even when she got the Professorship, there were only about five woman professors at UCC. Fortunately, her medical colleagues were most helpful, supportive and accommodating.

As Acting Head of the College of Medicine & Health, she faced challenges during a recession period in terms of managing all the disciplines and in controlling staffing numbers and the budget.

OPPORTUNITIES THAT ENHANCED SUCCESS

Geraldine admits that she has been very fortunate with opportunities to work in Ireland, the UK, USA and Canada in a variety of clinical and hospital roles. In particular, working in leadership roles such as Research & Development Manager for Nursing at Beaumont Hospital, Dublin (1990 to 1994), as Lecturer and Founding Professor of Nursing at UCC (1994 to 2010), and as Head of the College of Medicine & Health at UCC (2010 to 2011) offered unlimited opportunities.

The opportunity to be a member of national and local Committees, most of which were Ministerial nominations, also enhanced her success. She was a member of the Southern Health Board; the Tallaght Hospital Board; the Commission on Nursing; the Education Forum; the National Implementation Committee for undergraduate BSc nurse education; the Expert Group and National Implementation Committee direct entry programmes in Midwifery & Children's Nurse Education and the Task Force on

Undergraduate Medical Education; the Health Information & Quality Authority (HIQA); and the Fulbright Commission.

OBSTACLES ENCOUNTERED AND LESSONS LEARNED

People with a different perspective sometimes presented obstacles when working with change. However, she found ways around people: one of the ways she reveals is to express your opinion such that people eventually think it is their own idea.

She describes also the importance of distancing oneself from an issue – this skill comes with time and experience. She thinks change management, in particular, is easier if you are an outsider.

She has realised over the years that she has the ability and skills to find ways around obstacles. For example, when she wanted the Department of Nursing to become a School of Nursing, the then Registrar was not convinced. So she got permission to bring in a professor from the UK, Jane McFarland, a formidable woman. Following a report that Professor McFarland wrote, changes started to take place. Geraldine's advice is to keep at it until the desired outcome is achieved.

ADVICE TO ASPIRING LEADERS

Geraldine's advice to aspiring leaders is to know yourself and what motivates you, and to expose yourself to all possible experiences.

She recommends looking for opportunities where you can use your skills and competencies. She advocates educating yourself to the highest possible level. Making decisions based on factual information is paramount. She advises building teams of people and allocating work based on capacity.

Networking outside your own circle, and seeing whether you can get into that bigger circle, even if it means getting involved in a political party or onto executive boards, is essential.

Finally, she advises that "If you don't have resilience, develop it". She feels that, with resilience, comes commitment. She mentions also the ability to depersonalise experiences and not being offended or shocked.

Her key message to aspiring leaders, however, is to find a balance between life and work.

CHAPTER 16
KATHLEEN MURPHY

Patricia Leahy-Warren

An ability to be strategic, analytical, tenacious and resilient.

Kathleen Murphy is the founding Professor and Head of the School of Nursing & Midwifery at the National University of Ireland Galway (NUIG). Kathy holds a Bachelor's degree in Anthropology, History and English, a Master's Degree in Nursing and a PhD from Trinity College Dublin (TCD).

She is a native of Belfast and has spent many years as a nurse, nurse teacher and lecturer in the United Kingdom (UK).

She was a member of the Education Forum; the National Implementation Committee for undergraduate BSc nurse education; and the Expert Group and National Implementation Committee direct entry programmes in Midwifery & Children's Nurse Education.

Her research is focused on eldercare and she has led a number of research projects. She has presented and published her work internationally.

EARLY INFLUENCES

Kathy was born in Belfast and moved to England in 1969. This was the beginning of 'the Troubles' in Northern Ireland when many families had to leave their homes. She described this period in her life as difficult and family life as challenging.

Kathy always wanted to be a nurse but circumstances dictated that she had to leave school at 15, so studying nursing posed a challenge. On moving to England, she worked in an office but nursing was always what she really wanted to do. She identified a pre-nursing scheme as an entry route into nursing for people without formal educational qualifications and, through this, entered nurse training.

One of the early influences in her nurse training was a ward sister whose ward was well-managed; no tasks were ever left undone. Her organisational skills were exemplary but staff and patients were very fearful of her. Kathy struggled with the lack of a person-centred philosophy and realised that nursing structures were such that care was about tasks, routine and tidiness. While the care was considered exemplary at the time, patients were frequently scared of the ward sister, and emotional needs often were neglected. The lack of focus on the person, the hierarchical structures, attention to petty details and powerlessness had a major impact on Kathy. For that reason, she decided at the end of her training to leave nursing.

Kathy pursued a degree in Anthropology, History and English, with a view to becoming a teacher. In the last year of her degree, however, she worked part-time as a registered nurse in older people services. She was approached by the Director of Nursing of the Unit to consider applying for the night sister's position and her application was successful. This post allowed her to have a key role in influencing patient care, gave her the opportunity to introduce change and had a key impact on Kathy's decision to remain in nursing. Kathy felt she went from being powerless as a student to a position where she could influence and improve clinical practice and patient care.

It was during this time that she first encountered Barbara Vaughan and Sue Pembury, who were very influential figures in nursing in the UK. They believed that a hierarchical approach was not conducive to getting the best from people. The approach they took was to flatten hierarchies totally and thus open up opportunities for everybody to get involved, and allowing creativity and innovation to shine. Whilst some people excelled through this approach, others who had held senior positions within hierarchical structures became disempowered and thus became very disaffected. This taught Kathy that leadership is ensuring that vision and structures are in place to make sure that everybody has a role and a sense of purpose.

Vaughan and Pembury also were instrumental in Oxford in developing new and innovative approaches to care of older people, thus contributing to nursing practice and improving patient care. Barbara Vaughan went on to become the Director of Nursing Developments Programme in the Royal College of Nursing (RCN) in conjunction with the King's Fund. She was instrumental in developing the lecturer-practitioner role, in direct response to the need for clinical credibility in addressing the disparity between theory and practice.

MAJOR LIFE EVENTS

Kathy moved from Oxford to Essex where she attained a post in Epping. She held the post as a senior sister for five years. To facilitate family care, she put structures and systems in place to ensure holistic nursing care was delivered.

It was at this time she realised that, in fact, teaching the students and shaping how they viewed nursing was important to her. She was funded to undertake a Diploma in Nursing and a Nurse Tutors course, and worked for a year in the School of Nursing in Epping before taking a job as Lecturer-Practitioner at Oxford Brooks University. Subsequently she was appointed a lecturer at the School, which started to offer degree-only education to students. The School was a very democratic place, which allowed people to take on roles unfettered by hierarchy and to pursue and engage in pursuits that contributed to individual career ambitions. Kathy believes this was an important lesson in her career as a leader, as she realised the importance of giving people opportunity. She worked closely with staff in developing degree programmes for nurses. During her 10 years' tenure, she progressed to Deputy Head of the School of Nursing.

She had responsibility, together with two other lecturers, for reorganising the school, which had 160 staff, and for introducing new structures and systems. This position facilitated her professional development in management and leadership and enabled her to apply for, and be successful in securing, the leadership role as Director of Nursing Studies in NUIG.

VISION FOR YOUR LIFE'S WORK

Being autonomous and having the freedom to make one's own choices is very important to Kathy. She found that the university structures facilitated this freedom. Kathy believes that allowing people to make their own decisions on how to work results in a greater output. She has a preference for this style of leadership in facilitating staff development, enabling them to make choices rather than actually imposing choices on people.

What has motivated her throughout her career is her absolute belief that nursing is about working with people to help them care for themselves. Education and research is a fundamental component of this.

She believes that a research agenda within the School of Nursing is absolutely essential to be recognised by peers across the university. Her key research strategy was to seek funding for large research projects that would improve patient care outcomes. This she has achieved with a number of Health Research Board-funded multidisciplinary projects. These include the Dementia Education Programme incorporating Reminiscence Therapy for Staff (DARES) and the PRINCE study examining the impact of a pulmonary rehabilitation programme incorporating a behaviour change component for people with chronic obstructive pulmonary disease (COPD). She also worked with the National Council of Ageing & Older People (NCAOP) on a number of research projects.

CHARACTERISTICS OF LEADERS

To be visionary; to see what needs to be done in the future; and to be able to motivate and engage people sufficiently with the delivery of that vision.

SIGNIFICANT CHALLENGES

Kathy considerers the greatest challenge to date in her career was in establishing the School of Nursing Studies in NUIG. The move of nurse education from the School of Nursing in the health sector to third-level institutions necessitated negotiation between the University and the School. Relationships were very strained at times, yet a curriculum had to be developed and delivered across both institutions. As a leader, Kathy was challenged by the local politics and the different cultures of the two institutions.

Two main strategies contributed to the successful outcome. One was to ensure all staff who transferred from the School to the University were made very welcome and given opportunities and responsibilities. The second was to ensure the integration of established and transferring staff; this was facilitated partly by open-plan offices, which increased communication and created opportunities for sharing.

OPPORTUNITIES THAT ENHANCED SUCCESS

Kathy attributes her career success to her ability to be strategic, analytical, tenacious and resilient. She sets goals and targets that are realistic and achievable and works well through people.

Her early childhood was influential in developing her resilience and sense of self. Over the years, she has always been encouraged by her husband to believe in herself and her abilities to succeed. Kathy also believes that her personal life and work experiences have fostered her empathetic skills in being able to support people.

She embraces a challenge and has the analytic ability to see the parts of the whole in putting things together as a package to facilitate getting things done.

A key strength for Kathy is her family, who give a focus to her life outside of work. She stressed the importance for women, in particular, to have friends, outside interests and family, to give meaning to one's life.

Kathy's clinical and managerial skills were recognised by nurse leaders and she was encouraged to apply for senior posts very early in her career. Her success was built on success, with her drive and motivation to develop her career. Her belief in her own abilities was mirrored by the belief of her employers, who funded her ongoing professional development and education to undertake Diploma, Master's and PhD degrees. Securing a post in Oxford Brookes University in such a creative place at the right time was very important and contributed to her career progression.

OBSTACLES ENCOUNTERED AND LESSONS LEARNED

Kathy readily admitted that she has learned from mistakes made throughout her career. She admits to constantly taking on more work than she has the time for and, when newly appointed to a management position, to dealing with an issue in the heat of the moment without the benefit of reflection.

One mistake that she learned from was to allow two separate groups to be formed within her unit when she was ward sister in Accident & Emergency. Within each group, individuals worked together and because they had the same week-ends off-duty, they socialised together, often to the exclusion of the other group. This created a division between the groups when it came to development issues. She believes that people who work together, undertaking common tasks, have much more tolerance of each other as they have a greater understanding of each other. It is important therefore to ensure people have opportunities to work between, as well as within, groups. So, in the School of Nursing & Midwifery, everybody teaches across all undergraduate and postgraduate programmes so that there are no cliques.

ADVICE TO ASPIRING LEADERS

Advice for aspiring leaders includes career planning; the support of a mentor; be ambitious; do not be afraid to fail; be organised and you can have a career and a family.

Nurses need to believe in themselves, to apply for positions and to take risks. Kathy also believes there is a gender issue, in that men are more ambitious and willing to apply for a position much earlier in their career than women. Career mentoring, therefore, is really important for women.

CHAPTER 17
SIOBHAN O'HALLORAN

Sandra Swanton

*If your actions inspire others to dream more, learn more, do
more and become more, you are a leader.*

Siobhan O'Halloran is Assistant National Director for Acute
Hospital Services for Palliative Care, Integrated Services
Directorate, in the Health Service Executive. She is a Registered
Nurse in Intellectual Disability and a Registered General Nurse. She
holds a BSc in Nursing, a Post-graduate Diploma in Statistics, and a
MSc and PhD. She has completed a Fellowship in Nursing &
Midwifery, and a Professional Programme in Leadership.

Siobhan has held posts as Head of the School of Nursing, Midwifery, Health Studies & Applied Science at Dundalk Institute of Technology; Project Officer with the Health Services Reform Office, with specific responsibility for the action groups on the Health Information & Quality Authority (HIQA); Executive Director of the National Implementation Committee (Pre-registration Nursing Degree Programme); Nurse Advisor (education/research/intellectual disability) with the Department of Health & Children; and as a Lecturer with Dublin City University.

She has served on a number of national committees and completed a term of office as Chairperson of the Expert Group on Midwifery & Children's Nursing Education.

EARLY INFLUENCES

Siobhan began school at a very young age. She worked hard at subjects she found interesting and challenging and excelled in some areas, particularly at Latin.

Siobhan's choice of nursing was related to early experiences of working with individuals with an intellectual disability. Choosing this area of nursing was to influence Siobhan throughout her career. She credits a nurse tutor as having a very positive influence on her early career. This tutor was extremely engaging in her way of thinking and her teaching was interactive. The reading on the disability course was diverse and exposed Siobhan to a wide variety of subjects that she found fascinating.

MAJOR LIFE EVENTS

The person that Siobhan singles out as playing a major influential role in her professional life was the first Chief Nurse in Ireland. She describes her as having a way of managing so that, if someone was enthusiastic about work and they were motivated, they could do anything they wanted to do. The only time that anyone had to refer to the Chief Nurse was if they had made a mistake – and then she would fix it. Or if the system was blocked, she would unblock it so that they could continue their work. Siobhan says that this Chief Nurse's leadership skills and management style have definitely influenced the way that she now works and manages.

The other person who also was very influential was the Director of one of the Institutes of Technology where Siobhan was Head of Faculty. Again, it was about his leadership style and his absolute belief that anything was possible. If someone pointed out to him what they felt the blocks were, he was a person that could just unblock a system and never try to manage or control in any way. In selecting people to work with her, Siobhan says that it is people like that she is particularly interested in. If people need supervision, she says it really would not work out, because she just would not be there to do it. What works for her team is that, if someone runs into problems, they identify these to her and she does what she can to sort them out so that the person can continue to work autonomously. This is the way she operates in her current role. She considers that both the first Chief Nurse and the Director of the Institute of Technology were major influences in this respect.

VISION FOR YOUR LIFE'S WORK

Siobhan's vision for her life's work is to develop and progress the nursing and midwifery professions. She started working in the Department of Health as a nursing advisor 13 years ago and thinks that people consider that she can be relied on to give professional advice without a hidden agenda. Her work in the Department was to identify where nursing needed to be and then to try to lead nursing into those spaces. She had a very strong collaborative working circle that involved the major stakeholders. Despite this, she says she probably will be remembered for changing practice to support service delivery.

COMPETENCIES, STRENGTHS AND VALUES

Siobhan's understanding of human nature is something that she obtained from her experience in intellectual disability nursing. Values appreciated are recognising the individuality of every person; recognising talent, and trying to capitalise on that talent and enable that person to play to their talents. Her competence in the main relates to her capacity to get things done, make things happen and engage large groups of people to achieve this.

She considers that patience and tolerance are other strengths. Another important strength is the capacity to work out where nursing needs to be brought to, by understanding and interpreting what is happening internationally – for example, the expansion of nursing practice into nurse prescribing. She remains aware and keeps abreast of nursing development around the world by continuously reading and interacting internationally. When she sees the opportunity arising here in Ireland to implement whatever initiative it is, then everything is ready to make it happen.

During the Commission of Nursing, one of the things that needed to happen was education to degree level. The Commission became the vehicle to make that happen. In more recent years, nurse prescribing was recognised as an initiative that could enhance patient care.

It is about being ready to visualise, act and move. Siobhan emphasises the need to ensure that she understands the next event that needs to happen in nursing so that she can lead the initiative.

CHARACTERISTICS OF LEADERS

Siobhan says a leader is somebody who can create a vision and bring about change. Leaders have a charisma that ensures followership and have the capacity to unblock a system and allow people to become the best that they can become and to do the best that they can do. The ability to hold a team together is also vital.

As a leader, one has to continuously reflect, to have a good sense of humour and not to take yourself too seriously. You need some degree of imagination and creativity; you need to be able to dream out the future.

Confident and intelligent risk-taking and knowing how to live with failure are also important.

Good leadership is about supporting people, and about recognising when certain decisions just have to be made. "Critical to good strong leadership is the ability to make difficult decisions and to stand confidently and say we are now moving in this direction. In leadership, our actions should inspire people to dream more and to believe that they can move even further than where you've lead them".

SIGNIFICANT CHALLENGES

Siobhan has moved between different organisations throughout her career and says that learning to deal with the different cultures has been a major challenge. She remembers when she started as a student on the nursing degree programme. She knew absolutely nothing about the programme and really grappled with it for the first couple of weeks. Everyone else on the course seemed to know exactly what was going on and she says that she just watched to see how they interacted and, in this way, learned how to cope with the programme.

She has not spent any longer than two to four years in any job. She likes change and challenge. Moving around between organisations, she says, gives one a wonderful learning experience and understanding of the different facets of nursing, but it is a challenge to learn the different cultures and how to work within different organisations.

Other challenges outside of work include climbing to base camp Everest and challenging herself to move on; also climbing Table Mountain in South Africa. Challenges motivate her. She considers that challenges are key to her success and says the higher the bar is set, the better. She strives to succeed beyond expectations.

OPPORTUNITIES THAT ENHANCED SUCCESS

Siobhan cites the opportunity to attend college when she was 30 as being the opportunity that has most enhanced her, both personally and professionally. She considers that the timing was perfect, as before this she was too busy doing other things. She was intellectually ready for it and spent the next 10 years involved in academia. She published during this time and says that it was a fantastic opportunity and certainly shaped her career and enhanced her success.

The second event that shaped her career was the opportunity to work with the Department of Health & Children. She says that this opportunity gave her a completely different understanding of where nursing was, and how to bring about national change. Amongst other things, she learned to understand the industrial relations process and the role of the trade union. She says that the smartest people she ever worked with in her life have been in the Department of Health & Children.

Siobhan also worked in a Children's Hospital in Bucharest just after Ceausescu was shot. She found that an extraordinary opportunity because there was no shape or structure in place, there was nobody running the hospital, nobody interested in it. The children were in their cots and starving. So the opportunity was there just to walk in and do the best she could for the time she was there. This experience gave her confidence and taught her how to rely on her own strengths. That opportunity stands out as being the most rewarding of her career.

OBSTACLES ENCOUNTERED AND LESSONS LEARNED

Siobhan sees her main obstacles in terms of personal weaknesses. She comments that some mistakes have been made because of communication errors or because she is moving and thinking so fast. Once she has achieved something, it holds no interest for her. She has now learned to surround herself with people who are good communicators, using talents that she does not have herself.

In relation to lessons learned, she says she frequently asks herself questions about leadership.

ADVICE TO ASPIRING LEADERS

Siobhan's advice is dream the absolute impossible; to make a difference; and to create an unimaginable future for nursing and go pursue it.

Siobhan believes that re-engineering the nursing profession is in part a major solution to managing and re-organising the current health services.

CHAPTER 18
ANNE O'MAHONY

Elizabeth O'Connell

Be clear about where you are going and what you want to do.

Anne O'Mahony is Country Director of Concern Worldwide, an international, humanitarian organisation dedicated to poverty eradication and humanitarian relief in the world's poorest countries. She has overseen relief and development operations in Africa and Asia.

Anne is a Registered General Nurse and holds a Master's in Development Economics and Planning from the University of

Swansea. She has co-ordinated several non-government organisation (NGO) responses to humanitarian crisis. For 30 years, Anne has been involved in providing emergency food aid, support services and long-term development in countries such as Ethiopia, Cambodia, Sudan, Somalia, Rwanda, Liberia, Sierra Leone and, most recently, Kenya. She was a member of the Executive Committee of the Cambodian Co-ordination Committee, chaired the NGO forum in Rwanda and represented NGOs that were not officially associated with Operation Lifeline in Sudan at the Operation Lifeline Sudan Forum in Nairobi, Kenya.

She was a member of the Advisory Board for Development Cooperation Ireland (ABDCI) and Vice President of EuronAid, a European NGO food security network based in The Hague up to 2008.

EARLY INFLUENCES

Anne always wanted to work overseas and knew a career as a nurse or a teacher would make this easier. She was aware of the world outside of Ireland from an early age. Missionaries came regularly to her primary school and they generated a sense of excitement and adventure in a world outside Ireland. Her uncle, who was a priest in Birmingham, used to have the children of the family write Christmas cards to Amnesty Prisoners of Conscience when they were just seven or eight years of age, sending letters to such exotic locations as Russia, Nicaragua and Chile.

MAJOR LIFE EVENTS

There was no major event but early work with Concern influenced where she is placed today. Anne began work with Concern in 1982 and intended returning to Ireland after two years and settling down to a permanent pensionable job in Cork. Her first job was working with refugees on the Thai-Cambodian border and, a year later, she went to Ethiopia when a famine was just beginning. Due to illness, she returned to Ireland for a short while and then the Ethiopian famine hit the headlines. A rapid recovery meant she was able to go back to Ethiopia where she stayed for two years. It was challenging and personally-rewarding work but, at times, heartbreaking. She worked in famine relief centres and eventually moved into management so that, by 1986, she became Assistant Country Director.

A crossroads in her career was reached in 1987, when An Bord Altranais introduced the live register (with a fee involved). She wondered whether she should go home and maintain her registration as a nurse or make a life in overseas development her career. She had been able to take an extended leave of absence from the hospital in Cork, which gave a certain sense of security but, by 1987, nursing on a ward in Ireland was not what she thought her future would be and she finally made the decision to remain in overseas work. She resigned from her position and moved to Somalia. In 1989, she took up the post of Country Director in Sudan.

In 1993, she completed a Master's in Development Economics and Planning at Swansea University. Although she had worked at management level in Sudan, Somalia and Ethiopia, she felt she needed the degree for credibility.

VISION FOR YOUR LIFE'S WORK

Her vision is a job that is stimulating and fulfilling. Never in 30 years has her job been boring or even repetitive.

Anne has a strong belief in the work of Concern and its focus on the alleviation of poverty. Her work is to contribute as much as she can to this poverty alleviation goal. A lot can be done through innovative programming and she has been privileged to see many successes over the years.

COMPETENCIES, STRENGTHS AND VALUES

Anne's biggest strength is the recognition that she cannot do everything herself. She recognises that there are people better at doing certain things. She sees her job as the conductor of an orchestra, bringing everyone together to do what they are best at, to enable people to achieve a good collective result. Many skilled and motivated people are needed in response to any crisis, to set up nutrition interventions, organise schedules, open supply routes, set up sanitation and water facilities. They can work effectively only if they have the space and scope to work. Her job is to create and manage that space.

Nursing has always been her foundation. She believes her background in health has been a tremendous benefit to her work. Nursing gives her a broad perspective. Her colleagues in Concern often say that nurses are invaluable in any emergency situation due to their practical commonsense approach and their ability to tackle a large variety of tasks, way outside the comfort zone. Nurses are just as comfortable organising the loading of a truck or the digging of a well as setting up a primary healthcare or nutrition centre.

Many of the programmes that Anne designs and manages are health-related, in the field of primary healthcare and nutrition.

CHARACTERISTICS OF LEADERS

An ability to inspire the members of the team to achieve more collectively than any one of them can achieve individually is key. Effective leadership can get the best out of people and unlock hidden potential.

Important characteristics include excellent communication skills, clarity in strategy, and the ability to communicate clearly to the team. The use of persuasion to get people 'on board' is also essential.

SIGNIFICANT CHALLENGES

Being a woman was a challenge, and certainly being a woman in management was a significant challenge in many of the countries Anne has worked in. She has had to work harder than male counterparts to overcome these challenges; go to meetings more prepared and speak with greater authority; persist in requesting meetings with government officials; and prove that nothing phased or scared her. This included working in warzones, where her biggest challenge was ensuring that the team survived each day in the midst of gunfire, mayhem and famine.

It also included visiting a prison of over 8,000 men in post-genocide Rwanda, where the men were in an open space behind a high wall and she was the only woman. There were no prison guards when the huge door was closed behind her, locking her in with them. After a moment of sheer panic, she stiffened her spine, smiled politely and one of the prisoners stepped forward to show her around ... panic over.

As she has gotten older, these challenges have diminished. Age seems to imply knowledge and authority. She feels she no longer has to fight for recognition and it is easier to open doors.

OPPORTUNITIES THAT ENHANCED SUCCESS

Anne believes that you have to take advantage of opportunities as they arise in order to achieve goals. She remembers in particular the development of Community Therapeutic Care (CTC). Up to 1999, malnourished children came into feeding centres with their mothers or carers for periods of up to eight weeks before they were strong enough to return to their homes. This meant that the mother (who might have had five or six other children and many responsibilities such as collecting water and firewood, preparing food, looking after crops or going to market) was removed from her community for a long period of time, to devote all her attention to one child. She felt this created undue hardship for families and communities. Concern decided to look at this practice and see how it could be improved.

At the time, a new product called Plumpy'nut became available, which had the potential to be very effective in the treatment of malnutrition in children. Using this product, Concern developed the CTC protocol for treating malnutrition, which reversed global conventional thinking and, with Valid International, a research institution, demonstrated that it was a much more effective way of treating these very ill children. Mothers and their children would no longer need to leave their communities in order to be treated.

She is very proud of this achievement, a paradigm shift in the way global acute malnutrition (GAM) and severe acute malnutrition (SAM) is being dealt with. It has now been written into the World Health Organization's *Guidelines for the Treatment of Malnutrition* and also has been adopted by the Ministry for Health in Kenya and elsewhere around the world. She sits in meetings and hears French, Belgian, Kenyan and American experts, all talking about their CTC interventions, knowing Concern's role in this. It is an example of taking advantage of a new development or opportunity in order to improve care.

Emerging technologies are providing huge opportunities to work more efficiently to reach more people and alleviate poverty. Other opportunities Anne has been able to take advantage of involve the use of technology – for instance, in Kenya, mobile phones can now be used to transfer money. Concern was the first organisation in the world to use this technology in an emergency response to get money into the hands of the extremely poor, following post-election violence in Kenya in early 2008.

OBSTACLES ENCOUNTERED AND LESSONS LEARNED

In many countries, people may call themselves nurses after two weeks' training. Anne stated her professional background in nursing did not open any doors. In her first job as Country Director for Concern, she needed props and supports. After two years in Sudan as a woman in her early 30s and stating nursing as her professional background and feeling a bit inadequate, she struggled desperately to try to cover that inadequacy. After Sudan, she did a Master's degree in Development Economics to try and combat this. Interestingly, when she did not have a Master's, she felt it was a major constraint and thought she could not function without it. Once she got it, she never had to use it to boost her credibility. It was a confidence thing but she enjoyed the study nevertheless.

She is consistently challenged to do the right thing and there can be barriers that need to be broken down in order to achieve goals. Sometimes, a programme intervention can have unintended adverse consequences on the extremely vulnerable. An example of this is that, at the moment, she is campaigning to move the Dandora dump (an open dump with 170,000 people living around it, all struggling to survive) from the middle of a slum in Nairobi. Health and sanitation hazards are huge. Rats thrive and birds of prey, such as the very ugly marabou stork, are there in huge numbers. There is a constant haze of acrid smoke over the slum. At last, it looks as if the dump is actually going to be moved. But there are thousands of families who comb the dump and sell everything from plastic bags to empty bottles and who will lose their livelihoods once the dump is moved. They have no other way of earning a living and, without any form of social welfare in Kenya, their future looks grim. While the lives of many will be improved with the closure of the dump, she and others at Concern now must look at this core group and help them with training programmes, job-finding and setting them up in their own small businesses.

ADVICE TO ASPIRING LEADERS

Be clear about where you are going or what you want to do, and communicate this clearly to your team in order to inspire them. Use persuasion to address dissenting voices but always be prepared to listen to other viewpoints. Be prepared to go outside your comfort zone.

CHAPTER 19
ROSEMARY RYAN

Alice Coffey

Never become tunnel-visioned in nursing but look outside and
see how others do their work.

Rosemary Ryan is Risk & Compliance Manager with the Irish
Public Bodies Mutual Insurances Ltd.

She studied paediatric nursing at Our Lady's Hospital, Crumlin,
general nursing at St James's Hospital, Dublin and midwifery in
England. She holds a Higher Diploma and BA degree in health
service management, as well as Master's degrees in project

management and in environmental health and safety risk management.

She worked as a midwife and labour ward sister at the National Maternity Hospital in Dublin for 11 years. In 1998, she became Director of Nursing at St. James's Hospital, Dublin and worked with Ms. Peta Taaffe, the first Chief Nurse in the Department of Health & Children, and others in a campaign to raise awareness of managing clinical risk in the Irish health services.

Other posts she held include: Nurse Manager of Women's & Children's Services in 1991 at Altnagelvin Hospital in Derry, Northern Ireland; Director of Patient Services and Head of Nursing, and later as Executive Director, at Altnagelvin National Health Service (NHS) Trust. In this last role, Rosemary had responsibility for a £48 million capital development programme and introduced the first quality and clinical risk management programme in Northern Ireland.

She attributes her success to the principles of her nursing background, her motivation to learn, facilitative leadership and openness to change.

EARLY INFLUENCES

Rosemary acknowledges that, in her early life, she had no academic aspirations, assuming that nursing was beyond her capability. However, the achievement of good results in her secondary school examinations caused her to change her mind and turn her attention towards nursing as a career choice.

Rosemary's father had been a psychiatric nurse before she was born and her mother had three sisters who were nurses. However, she distinctly remembers that her father did not approve of her aspirations for nursing. He was of the opinion that it was too difficult a job for a lady. At school, Rosemary found similar attitudes toward nursing from career guidance teachers. Students were encouraged to become teachers or to enter a career in the civil service, as nursing was not considered suitable. Nonetheless,

Rosemary was not deterred. At first, she applied to St. Michael's Hospital in Dun Laoghaire, Dublin for combined training in general and psychiatric nursing. Her recollection of the application process includes the completion of an essay titled, *All work and no play make Jack a dull boy*, where she shared some of her early insights into what is now termed 'work-life balance'. Although the Matron of St. Michael's was impressed by her essay and offered her a place, Rosemary declined as she had children's nursing in mind. A short time later, she commenced a combined children's and general nursing programme at Our Lady's Hospital, Crumlin, with general nurse training delivered at St James's Hospital.

Another influence towards a nursing career was Rosemary's involvement in caring for her father, who suffered from a chronic illness.

In her career development and her attitude to care delivery, Rosemary cites her experience of working with the late Dr. John Stronge, Master of the National Maternity Hospital, Holles Street, Dublin from 1984 to 1990, as a major influence, as was the influence of the hospital's Matron, Miss Una Murphy. She greatly admired the openness and transparency with which Dr. Stronge delivered care to his patients. On occasions when the management of labour did not work out as expected for a woman in his care, Dr. Stronge would conduct a review of care and decision-making to identify problems and reasons for decisions made. He readily admitted mistakes directly to the woman and encouraged the midwives to do likewise. This approach also was supported by the hospital's Matron. In Dr. Stronge's opinion, women were entitled to know the reasons behind clinical decisions that affected them. Rosemary described Dr. Stronge as someone who discussed issues with women regarding their care and expectations with humanity and compassion.

Rosemary's career and leadership style was influenced later by the Chief Executive Officer (CEO) of the Northern Ireland NHS Trust where she worked as a Director of Patient Services from 1991 to 1997. The CEO, who was an accountant, was always open to new ideas and possibilities. He taught Rosemary the fundamentals of planning and systems thinking. His leadership style was facilitative and included an open-door policy to promote coaching and mentoring.

MAJOR LIFE EVENTS

The loss of her father was a major life event for Rosemary and the chronic nature of his illness meant that she had become increasingly involved in his care during her early nursing career. Some experiences during this time helped to shape her style of leadership and management. On one occasion, Rosemary was informed that her father had become ill and that there was the distinct possibility that he might not survive long. She promptly requested time off to be with him but hospital management refused to grant it. Because her father's condition deteriorated so rapidly, and having observed that her ward was adequately staffed, she informed hospital management of her decision to leave to be with him. She was informed that, if she left the hospital, she could not return. Her father's condition stabilised overnight and Rosemary returned to work the following day. Although she experienced no immediate consequences, this incident resonated with Rosemary throughout her career. She resolved that she would never deny someone the opportunity to be with a significant person at a crucial time in their lives.

When her father died a short time later, her compassionate leave was reduced by one day in lieu of the time she had previously left the hospital. Following this major event in her personal life, Rosemary recalls receiving little understanding from nursing management. Although she acknowledges that, at the time, nurse managers were "fine people", they were reluctant to display humanity to their staff and lacked some basic skills in interpersonal communication. This became an important milestone in Rosemary's learning and a lesson for her future career in nurse management.

Her move to Stoke-on-Trent in England to study midwifery, in 1979, during the height of 'the Troubles' in Northern Ireland, changed Rosemary's understanding of difference in perspective. This was immediately after the Birmingham bombing and this event, along with the increasing violence in Northern Ireland, regularly led to patients (many of whom had relatives serving as soldiers) refusing care from Irish nurses. Rosemary acknowledges that, being young, she did not have much insight into the mindset of the people concerned. Yet her experiences led her to a greater understanding of diversity in personal and cultural perspectives in her future career.

In England, Rosemary observed that the learning environment for students was very different from that in Dublin. The culture was one of support and encouragement of expression. Students were 'matched up' with qualified staff who 'looked after' their clinical learning on the ward and acted as advisors and assessors of their progress, an arrangement later described as 'preceptorship'. Rosemary feels that her student experience in England taught her a different level of respect for students: to value the contribution of students to patient care.

Rosemary commenced her work as a midwife at the National Maternity Hospital in Dublin. She had heard people talk of the hospital's reputation throughout Europe as a centre of excellence in maternity care and she wanted to work in this type of environment. The matron at that time was Una Murphy, whom she described as a strict task-master who ensured the highest standards of midwifery practice while, at the same time, being very supportive of her staff, encouraging them to move forward in their careers.

Rosemary later became the youngest ward sister ever appointed at the hospital. This she remembers as a major challenge, as she had to deal with human resource issues for the first time, not knowing the correct method of dealing with them. This prompted Rosemary to seek out and engage in further education in management, to better understand the social, political and economic components of health service management. This management education provided her with new insights into the competencies required, such as knowledge regarding health services funding and alternative models of management.

Another major event in Rosemary's life was her move to work in Northern Ireland to take up the position as Manager of Women's & Children's Services in Derry. Rosemary found this challenging, both personally and professionally. Personally, she found it difficult to leave her mother who was then in her late 70s and a widow. Professionally, her responsibility in this new role extended beyond nursing to the management of all other clinical professions as well as administrative and support staff.

VISION FOR YOUR LIFE'S WORK

Rosemary always wanted to work alongside the best. She was motivated to develop her own knowledge by her pursuit of excellence. Her academic development was always self-directed and self-funded, with a view to understanding her role better and to becoming better equipped for new roles.

Although Rosemary has now left clinical nursing, she feels that she has brought the background and principles of nursing with her to all areas of her work. She believes that the skillset she built up in nursing and midwifery, and in management, has supported her throughout her career.

When opportunities presented themselves, Rosemary was willing to take them on. However, she acknowledges that her career was shaped also by the support and vision of good people she worked with, who saw her potential before she did.

COMPETENCIES, STRENGTHS AND VALUES

Rosemary believes that two of her greatest strengths – being a good observer and a good listener – can be linked back to her nursing career.

Observation of patterns of behaviour was always a key attribute in paediatric nursing. If observation was not at its highest level, consequences could be disastrous. Rosemary reflects on how this attribute assists her in her work today, in her ability to observe the presence of small problems in an organisation that can irritate people and cause unrest if nothing is done.

Rosemary has no problem giving time to people and is often commended for listening when nobody else does. In her experience, not enough time is afforded to people to express their grievances and issues either in public or private organisations. She feels that it is a terrible indictment of these organisations that many of their employees are experiencing difficulties but few are listened to.

Rosemary is a very good time manager. She admits to having a huge workload, estimating her output in one week to be equal to that of three risk managers. She believes in using resources conservatively in some ways but her ethos is to get the best added value out of the resources made available and the best return on investment possible.

CHARACTERISTICS OF LEADERS

The most important attributes of a good leader is to be facilitative of others; to be a team player; to lay out clearly expectations of outcomes and also to encourage delivery. If delivery of outcomes is not forthcoming, leaders should seek better ways of working so that achievements are realised.

Leaders should be aware of role descriptions and key performance indicators and know how best to communicate. This also means listening to others; this is frequently forgotten by leaders and managers.

OBSTACLES ENCOUNTERED AND LESSONS LEARNED

Rosemary recounted that one of the biggest challenges in her career was the cultural change that she encountered when she undertook her role as Director of Patient Services and Head of Nursing, and later as Executive Director of Nursing, in a Northern Ireland NHS Trust. The hospital had an innovative management structure and, although she was hungry to work in this dynamic and innovative environment, she was nervous of the political climate that existed. Rosemary found that the religious divide extended in a subtle manner to the boardroom, where meetings could be difficult to manage and, on occasion, consensus was difficult to achieve.

However, Rosemary learned some valuable lessons. For example, she learned that it is best to involve other members of the executive management team so as to share the governance for the planning and decision-making; also to talk to people first, to float new ideas and get each side's opinions and maybe their agreement before bringing the ideas to the table. These experiences taught Rosemary a new style of facilitative leadership, which she has maintained as her ethos since.

ADVICE TO ASPIRING LEADERS

Never take "No" for an answer without understanding the rationale. Listen to others; they may have the answer that you are looking for.

Know who you are to serve and do the right thing for others.

Keep your mind open and look outside your profession. New and useful ideas can emanate from outside the health sector that may improve it.

CHAPTER 20
ANNE SCOTT

Eileen Savage

*You can achieve pretty much anything you want if you
put your mind to it.*

Anne Scott is Deputy President and Registrar of Dublin City
University (DCU).

Anne trained as a general nurse in Sligo General Hospital. She
graduated with a primary degree in philosophy from Trinity
College Dublin, a Master's degree from the University of
Edinburgh, and a PhD from the University of Glasgow.

Prior to her current position, Anne was Professor of Nursing and Head of the School of Nursing at DCU for five years. Other appointments she held include: Senior lecturer in the Department of Nursing & Midwifery, University of Stirling, Scotland; Lectureships at Glasgow Caledonian University and the University of Glasgow; and clinical posts in Ireland and Kenya.

Anne's research interests are in the philosophy and ethics of healthcare, and judgement and decision-making. She publishes widely in the international literature and has a strong research profile, including funded projects and supervision of several doctoral students.

Anne has been appointed by the Minister of Health & Children to the Health Research Board and to the Board of the Health Services Executive. She is also a founding member of the Irish Council for Bioethics.

EARLY INFLUENCES

Anne's father was a small farmer and factory worker in County Cavan, who had no formal education beyond the age of 12. He taught Anne how to take responsibility for herself and her actions, and to do so with self-confidence and a questioning stance. The message that one's actions should not be a passive response to doing what one is told to do but rather an active and considered judgement about what is the best course of action in a given situation was instilled in Anne from a very early age. This message was repeated again and again by her father. Her father remains one of the most respected people in her life.

During Anne's secondary school years, a history teacher (Brendan McCann) was very influential by making scholarship visible. She recalled one incident in particular during a fourth year history class on the causes of the First World War. The history teacher gave the class four different books to read. The fact that experts on this topic differed substantially from one another provoked a sense of sheer excitement, which she believes has been greatly influential on developing her inquiring mind. This sense of excitement associated with differing arguments around knowledge continues to drive her research work to this day.

A third and major early influence on Anne's career was Mr. Joe Mullen, a principal nurse tutor whom she met when training to be a nurse in the late 1970s. He had a vision for nursing moving into the university sector and for developing as a scholarly discipline. Mr. Mullen exposed Anne to research and, within this context, encouraged students to question practices. He fostered Anne's love for research and evidence-based practice within a rich learning environment, including a small but well-resourced library that stocked nursing research monographs and papers. Anne became an avid reader of research, which heightened her awareness of the theory practice gap. This questioning stance has stayed with Anne ever since those earlier days on engaging with nursing research.

MAJOR LIFE EVENTS

Anne's mother died when she was six years old, following which her family emigrated to Canada. The family returned to Ireland when Anne was 10 years old. Being the oldest of a family of five children, Anne was placed in a position of responsibility for the domestic chores in the household and for minding her younger siblings while her father worked. This made Anne a very resilient person and she became accustomed to a considerable degree of autonomy – something she has continuously exercised throughout her working life.

Anne's academic education also was a major life event, especially in terms of how this has influenced her expectations of scholarship and research. Having qualified as a nurse, Anne pursued third-level education, starting with an undergraduate degree in philosophy and later undertaking a PhD degree. Being educated in well-established disciplines has provided her with a good overview of how disciplines knit together in the development of the history of ideas and knowledge. In addition, this education provided her with a contextualisation of the development of a discipline, especially philosophy. Anne sees nothing odd about nursing borrowing knowledge from other disciplines and likewise holds the view that nursing can contribute to other disciplines.

VISION FOR YOUR LIFE'S WORK

Scholarship and research lie at the heart of Anne's vision for her life's work. The pursuit of scholarship and research, whereby knowledge is developed, must be the fundamental reason why nursing as a discipline is situated in universities. While acknowledging that the development and delivery of educational programmes are integral to the business of universities, these activities do not justify integrating nursing into academia. Hospital-based Schools of Nursing historically have been very effective at delivering educational programmes without university influences. Therefore, there must be a very different reason for nursing being moved into universities – to engage in scholarship and research.

COMPETENCIES, STRENGTHS AND VALUES

Judgement and decision-making are core competencies required for leadership. Resilience is a strength needed to continuously push out boundaries and limitations, bring about change, and realise a vision for scholarship and research in nursing. Scholarship and research of international calibre is a deep-rooted value that Anne embraces for developing nursing as a discipline.

CHARACTERISTICS OF LEADERS

Characteristics of leaders are that they are visionary, energetic, have drive and ambition. To lead a team from one point to another, the leader's vision must be communicated to the entire team. Efforts at leadership are very likely to be ineffective if vision is not shared with the team. Clear communication is critical to getting a team to 'buy into' one's vision and to moving collectively towards realising that vision.

The leadership literature makes a contrast between leading from the front and leading from behind. This can be complex, however, because it requires a leader to be able to assess the strengths and weakness of a group of people in order to play to their strengths and support them to become *more* than they are. The level of support that individuals on a team need varies. A good leader is able to flex between the different strengths and weaknesses within the team. Irrespective of whether one is leading from the front or from behind, it is important to raise expectations of people and then help them to deliver on those expectations. This includes being there as a leader to pick up the pieces if mistakes are made by team members.

Although different approaches to leadership are used with different people according to their skillsets and abilities, the overall aim of keeping people together and working towards a shared direction and vision remains constant.

SIGNIFICANT CHALLENGES

Developing nursing as a scholarly discipline has presented significant challenges for Anne. When she moved from Scotland to Ireland to take up an academic appointment as Professor and Head of School at Dublin City University (DCU), nurse education was being fully integrated into the third-level sector and thereby became an all-graduate profession. This integration was onerous, requiring extensive consultations with internal and external stakeholders. In addition, the development of postgraduate educational programmes was high on the agenda of the management sector of the university. A vision for scholarship, foremost in Anne's mind, did not seem to be a priority among the various stakeholders. However, Anne refused to drop this vision, despite advice that scholarship and research needed to be 'put on the backburner' in order to meet the demands of progressing nurse education.

Anne's initial lead on scholarship was in the context of a very low base; staff capacity to engage in research was low and there was no evidence of emerging track records among staff. The School of Nursing was practically invisible within the university, with little or no recognition of it taking a place among other Schools towards excellence in scholarship and research. However, in Anne's mind, scholarship and research was going to become a reality in the School of Nursing, DCU, and this was 'absolutely not negotiable'. With Anne's lead, the School has been very successful as is evident in the growth of PhD students, and a growing track record of research and funding awards. A notable achievement has been the growth of over 50% of academic staff within the School to PhD level over a period of six to eight years – an achievement that has not been seen anywhere in the UK, even in the top universities such as King's College and Manchester.

Since Anne has moved from Head of School into her current positions as Deputy President and Registrar of DCU, she has had the opportunity to see how nursing is situated within the University as a whole. She is confident that nursing has been very effective in the growth of scholarship and research. The School's research track record has surpassed that of some established disciplines within the humanities and social sciences. Nursing on the whole, as a discipline and as a profession, has a vast intellectual resource that must be embraced. This remains a significant challenge for the development of nursing scholarship and research because its intellectual resource remains largely underused.

OPPORTUNITIES THAT ENHANCED SUCCESS

As Professor and Head of School, Anne led the School in an application for a nursing research grant. This marked the beginning of bringing staff forward in a collaborative exercise towards a common research goal – to conduct a study that was externally funded. Any member of staff who contributed to this application was acknowledged as a co-researcher. The application process was instrumental in shifting the School culture from no research activity to some activity such as literature searching, writing an application and budget planning. The School was successful in its application. The effects of this were very tangible in terms of empowering staff to engage in research and to promoting a belief in staff that they could become research-active. This funding opportunity generated a positive attitude among staff and a strong belief in their potential to compete nationally for funding and to grow as researchers.

ADVICE TO ASPIRING LEADERS

It is important to appreciate that leading from one point to another is not a linear process, and most often there is no direct route to realising one's vision. It is necessary to find the way to move forward and, to do this, one has to be able to read the signs and the cues that will contribute to progress. It is necessary to identify the 'power of aces' and negotiate one's way through.

Develop the self-confidence and resilience to push out and 'fight' any boundaries and limitations that are likely to halt progress and success in nursing. Do not let obstacles stifle one's judgement, and keep in mind that the most significant obstacles are often in one's own head.

Enhance people's expectations and support them in achieving these expectations.

Do not shy away from the risk of making mistakes – it is not possible to get it right all of the time.

A critical hallmark of successful leadership is to gain the respect and trust of people, and likewise to reciprocate a trusting and respectful relationship with these people.

CHAPTER 21
PETA TAAFFE

Margaret McKiernan

*It is a question of trying to bring people with you rather
than just telling them what to do.*

Peta Taaffe is now retired but was the first Chief Nurse of the
Department of Health & Children, a post she assumed in 1997. In
this position, Peta played a key role in implementing the
recommendations of the Commission on Nursing, including the
establishment of the Nursing Policy Division in the Department of
Health & Children; a new approach to workforce planning;
establishment of degree-level education for nurses nationally;
establishment of the National Council for the Professional

Development of Nursing & Midwifery; and development of clear career pathways for nurses in clinical practice, education and management.

She is a Registered General Nurse and Registered Midwife. She has held a number of posts as Matron in: Drogheda Cottage Hospital; Mercer's Hospital, Dublin; and the Royal City of Dublin Hospital, Baggot Street. Her last nursing management post in a hospital was as Director of Nursing at St. James's Hospital, Dublin.

She was a member of the Commission on Nursing; the Nurse Education Forum, and the National Implementation Committee for undergraduate BSc nurse education.

EARLY INFLUENCES

Peta wanted to study medicine initially but, for a variety of reasons, including finance and perception of women doctors at the time, she changed her mind and studied nursing. Her maternal aunt was a pioneering sort of nurse who worked in South America. Having been at school in England, she applied to the London teaching hospitals and trained as a nurse there.

Her father was not very impressed with her career choice. However, in the end, he was proud of Peta's achievements. Her father was very much a leader: he was in the Royal Air Force and, from the time Peta can remember, he commanded Royal Air Force air stations. Peta was aware that he did not lead from a distance but was present with his staff and respectful of them and their work.

MAJOR LIFE EVENTS

There were one or two people, especially from nursing, who helped to shape Peta's career.

A ward sister in a neurosurgical ward, who was always ready to listen, to correct and to respond quickly to patient's needs, was influential. Peta remembers her as being incredibly human, which was so important to the needs of her patients.

The midwives in the Labour Ward in Dumfries, where she trained as a midwife, were exceptional role models. One particular district midwife in Glasgow was very supportive always, coped with anything and everything, and was a wonderful teacher – nothing was impossible to her. With this midwife, Peta encountered undiagnosed twins, undiagnosed breeches, and houses with no indoor water or sanitation. This provided considerable learning opportunities.

VISION FOR YOUR LIFE'S WORK

Her vision included the wish to help patients, for nurses to be regarded as full members of the healthcare team and for the education for nurses to be at degree level. The last was necessary Peta felt, as in her day, student nurses were in charge of wards as second-year students but did not understand the risks involved. While some people may say that the nurse of today with degree-level education is not as good as the apprentice-style nurse, Peta disagrees and contends that, given experience, the degree-educated nurses are far better.

To advance and extend nursing roles to a level beyond the capabilities of junior doctors for the benefit of patient care was an aspiration. This she saw happen in St. James's, as she was Director of Nursing there when the first Emergency Nurse Practitioner was appointed.

Peta says nurses need to be more politically aware and work in a more cohesive group.

COMPETENCIES, STRENGTHS AND VALUES

The ability to bring people with you, rather than just telling them what to do is an important competency. The importance of communication, not accepting the *status quo* and making people part of the decision is vital.

Be organised; be present and seen; be reflective in decision-making; lead by example; respect others; and maintain a clinical awareness.

Be aware that subordinates sometimes can be in a stronger position than yourself. In reflecting on this, Peta instances an occurrence where a valued staff member was refused leave for a family occasion and, when refused, threatened to leave the organisation.

CHARACTERISTICS OF LEADERS

What is required is a certain amount of brass neck, empathy, humanity, an awareness of how people tick – what motivates them and what does not – and a basic belief in the goodness of human nature.

One has to want to be a leader at some level because people who do not want to be leaders do not do so well.

A mentor is useful, someone to bounce ideas off and discuss problems with.

A leader needs stamina, ambition, energy and sensitivity. Leaders need to be visible and use their professional background as required.

SIGNIFICANT CHALLENGES

Challenges Peta faced related to recruitment of sufficient staff with required competencies, especially in hard recession times or when the marriage bar applied (a law against hiring married women as permanent/tenured staff in State employment).

Selecting appropriate persons to fill posts was a challenge and one has to accept that you can never be right all of the time. Engaging senior staff in selection was a must for Peta.

Another challenge was working with an individual who undermined Peta all of the time. Peta found this very difficult and maintained that there are such people in organisations.

Very large challenges were encountered when Peta moved to the post as Chief Nurse in the Department of Health & Children. The position was new and the idea of civil servants working with nurses, in a time of exponential growth for the profession, was novel.

A challenge in the fast-moving health system is finding time to give safe care to patients.

Peta feels that unionised attitudes are a pity and that nurses need to present their own professional perspectives in a better manner.

OPPORTUNITIES THAT ENHANCED SUCCESS

Availability of a variety of posts to which Peta was recruited offered opportunities to advance. A management course at the Royal College of Nursing in London also enhanced her success as a manager and leader.

OBSTACLES ENCOUNTERED AND LESSONS LEARNED

Obstacles encountered relate to difficulties in recruiting persons to key clinical service posts.

Lessons were learned along the way and incorporated into practice.

One regret was the unavailability of degree-level education during Peta's formative years and, while she managed well without it, she lauds its introduction now for all nurses.

ADVICE TO ASPIRING LEADERS

Focus on the main task; be open to new ideas and opportunities as they present; listen to the people working with you; leave room for opportunity; and be prepared to acknowledge when people have better ideas that you do.

You must be interested in what is going on, enjoy your work and keep up-to-date with international best practice – in other words, be professional.

There must be an element of enjoyment and lightheartedness about being a leader. If you do not enjoy it most of the time, do not take it on.

CHAPTER 22
LESSONS LEARNED: PREPARING FUTURE LEADERS

Geraldine McCarthy and Joyce J. Fitzpatrick

This book consists of interviews with 20 women leaders who began their careers as nurses. Some have diversified and now lead important academic, health, social or entrepreneurial enterprises; there are 20 chapters based on interviews with such women.

Each interview was conducted in a format that provides information on: early influences; major life events; vision for life's work; competencies, strengths, and values; characteristics of leaders; significant challenges; opportunities that enhanced success; and advice to aspiring leaders. In the following paragraphs, we merge the information gathered to provide an overview of these key elements across the 20 interviews.

Early influences included those of parents who believed in education and professional careers for all family members. Siblings, friends, neighbours and work colleagues who encouraged were also important. Teachers with high standards and high expectations and nurses with expertise in communication, management and clinical ability were identified as influential. People who were trustful and those who listened and were attentive to aspirations were particularly important.

Major life events were parent or sibling deaths, love affairs that did not last, experiences working abroad and associated cultural experiences. Other events identified by the women leaders profiled were related to early nursing experiences, including challenges that helped them to discover their talents and abilities. Opportunities to represent nurses on a variety of governing bodies at various organisational and community levels were particularly influential.

Vision for life's work was to contribute to society, to give of oneself, including supporting others through a wide range of professional and personal activities. These core values permeated all participants' vision for their work. There was also an intention to deliver and manage service in a quality and safe manner. There was a belief in teams and the fact that one cannot work alone but instead needs the support and involvement of other individuals. There was an emphasis on the fact that people must learn to cope with failure, be ready and available for opportunities as they are presented and treat all people and situations on their own merits.

Competencies, strengths and values held by individuals across interviews can be summed up as having a helicopter view; using resilience; fairness; openness; the ability to listen; and the willingness to learn and work hard. Team-building; ethical stance; fact-selecting; decision-making; risk-taking; valuing others while recognising failures, but intolerance to inefficiencies and laziness were identified. The ability to learn and listen; to investigate situations thoroughly; and to be widely-read, intelligent, courageous, a good communicator and well-organised were important. Competencies also included a commitment to the devolvement of authority, an ability to step into the unknown and to make unpopular decisions when needed.

Leader characteristics that were perceived as important included: being fair; non-judgemental; strategic thinking; visionary; reflective; positive; challenging; inspiring; instilling hope; using opportunities; and knowing your business. A belief in yourself and in what you are doing; in being courageous; well-organised; respectful and accommodating of the views of others; a team-builder; and bearing no grudges but being able to move on after a disagreement were important characteristics identified.

Significant challenges included being a woman, often operating in a male-dominated environment. Achieving a work-life balance, experiencing personal illness, and direct clinical care involving traumatic situations were among the challenges cited. Time management; entrenched beliefs of other healthcare professionals; hierarchical structures; working towards accreditation; and the provision of funding were particularly challenging.

Opportunities that enhanced success included being in the right place at the right time; having a good education; being able to travel; and having the ability to identify excellent mentors. Leaders also identified professional opportunities, especially promotional opportunities and membership on boards, involvement in strategic planning and being lucky to have trained as a nurse as key to their success.

Obstacles encountered related to working with people with diverse opinions; the frustration experienced when one personally aims too high; management of difficult people; situations where there was no obvious learning from mistakes; and inappropriately trained people occupying posts. Not being listened to, a lack of vision among co-workers, and bureaucracy were encountered also.

Lessons learned and advice to aspiring leaders were as follows: distance yourself from the issue; express your opinions and give suggestions; let praise go to others if necessary; do not stand back; know yourself and what motivates you; look for opportunities where you can use your skills and competencies; be confident; have an ethical approach and be respectful of all people you encounter; be fair; find learning in rejection of your ideas; develop resilience; depersonalise issues; live a balanced life; commit to what you do; build teams and allocate work according to individual capacity; network outside your own discipline; educate yourself to the highest possible level and try to study with others; be well-researched; get a mentor; have a close friend; take risks; learn from failure; be political; be visible, organised, and flexible; use teams; do not expect people to be as enthusiastic as yourself; be an easy person to talk to; be non-judgemental; be caring. Many of these qualities are ones that are at the foundation of what was learned in nursing.

We hope in reading the stories that the reader will have learned about leadership and the influences on leadership. We want you to

be energised and motivated in your career and wish that you
would benchmark yourself against the experiences profiled and
find it a beneficial exercise.

THE EDITORS

Geraldine McCarthy PhD MSN MEd Dipn RNT RGN was founding Professor and Dean of the Catherine McAuley School of Nursing & Midwifery, which was established in University College Cork (UCC) in 1994. From 2010 to 2011, she held the post of Acting Head of the College of Medicine & Health at UCC, providing strategic leadership in research and educational programmes in Medicine,
Dentistry, Therapies, Pharmacy, Nursing and Midwifery.

She has held a variety of other positions in Ireland, the UK, USA and Canada. She holds a MEd from Trinity College Dublin (TCD), MSN and PhD degrees in Nursing from Case Western Reserve University, Cleveland, Ohio, USA. She has been a member of a number of national and EU bodies, including the Commission on Nursing, the Nurse Education Forum and the Task Force on undergraduate medical education. Currently, she is a Ministerial nominee to the Health Information & Quality Authority (HIQA) and to the Fulbright Commission.

She has published over 120 papers and has presented at national and international conferences. Her research interests include those associated with management and chronic disease self-care, especially in eldercare. She leads the Healthy Ageing Research Theme within the School and supervises both PhD and MSc Students. In addition, she is a member of the local Health Service Reconfiguration Team that is working to transform the Hospital & Community Health Services in the Southern Region.

Joyce J. Fitzpatrick PhD MBA RN FAAN FNAP is Elizabeth Brooks Ford Professor of Nursing, Frances Payne Bolton School of Nursing, Case Western Reserve University (CWRU) in Cleveland, Ohio, where she was Dean from 1982 through 1997. She holds an adjunct position as Professor, Department of Geriatrics, Mount Sinai School of Medicine, New York, NY.

She earned a BSN (Georgetown University), an MS in Psychiatric-Mental Health Nursing (Ohio State University), a PhD in Nursing (New York University), and an MBA (CWRU, 1992). In 1990, Dr. Fitzpatrick received an honorary doctorate, Doctor of Humane Letters, from her *alma mater*, Georgetown University and an honorary doctorate in 2011 from the Frontier University of Nursing. She served as a Fulbright Scholar at University College Cork (UCC), Cork, Ireland during 2007-2008, and has served as a consultant for publication and research development for UCC.

Professor Fitzpatrick has over 300 publications in nursing and healthcare, including 62 books that she has written or edited. She serves as editor of three major nursing journals: *Applied Nursing Research, Archives in Psychiatric Nursing,* and *Nursing Education Perspectives,* the official journal of the National League for Nursing.

THE CONTRIBUTORS

Vicki Cleary MSc BSc RGN PG Cert Teaching/Learning for Higher Education

Vicki has both medical and surgical nursing experience. She has a particular interest in gynaecological cancer care and lectures on the undergraduate BSc Nursing programme, Catherine McAuley School of Nursing & Midwifery, University College Cork (UCC).

Her research is focused on women's experiences of sexuality following a gynaecological cancer diagnosis. Vicki was awarded a three-year PhD studentship from the Catherine McAuley School of Nursing & Midwifery in 2009. Her PhD focuses on the development of a nursing intervention to address the sexuality of women with gynaecological cancer and is due for completion in 2012. She was awarded the European Oncology Nursing Society Major Research Grant in 2010 to support this research. She is a member of the European Academy of Nursing Science Doctoral Summer Schools and has presented at both national and international conferences.

Alice Coffey PhD MEd BA Health Management, RNT RGN RM

Alice is College Lecturer and Director of Post-graduate Programmes at Catherine McAuley School of Nursing & Midwifery, UCC.

Clinical experience includes Clinical Nurse Manager of a rehabilitation unit for older people.

Alice is lecturer and research supervisor on undergraduate and post-graduate programmes. Research interests are health and illness transitions for older adults. She was awarded a Clinical Research Fellowship from the Health Research Board to support her Ph.D. Currently, Alice is involved in research on Advanced Directives with the Department of Gerontology & Rehabilitation. Alice has published in international nursing journals.

She is a member of the UCC Ageing Research Cluster and the All Ireland Gerontological Nurses Association.

Nicola Cornally MSc BSc RGN Dip NS Cert in Nurse Management

Nicola is a PhD student and a Lecturer in Nursing at Catherine McAuley School of Nursing & Midwifery, UCC.

Nicola was employed previously as a research assistant at the School, where she was involved in many projects, including an exploration of the role of the practice nurse and the emergency nurse.

She is a Registered General Nurse with extensive clinical nursing experience and in practice development. Her research is focused on seeking help for chronic pain, with an emphasis on behavioural theory. Nicola was recently awarded a travel scholarship from the College of Medicine & Health to attend the European Pain Conference in Germany to present her work.

Patrick Cotter MSc BSc RGN RM RNP Dip Mgt PGDipN(A&E) Certificates in nurse prescribing of medicinal products and ionising radiation

Patrick is an Advanced Nurse Practitioner in Emergency Nursing at Cork University Hospital (CUH), Ireland and Adjunct Lecturer in Nursing at Catherine McAuley School of Nursing & Midwifery, UCC.

Previously, he worked as: Lecturer in Nursing, UCC; Clinical Nurse Manager, Emergency Department, South Infirmary/Victoria University Hospital, Cork; and various staff nurse positions.

He was a member of the National Resource & Implementation Group for Nurse Prescribing and is currently a member of the National Programme Board for Nurse Prescribing of Ionising Radiation. Patrick is the co-ordinator for the planning and implementation of reconfiguration of emergency care services in the Cork/Kerry region.

He has published on emergency and advanced nursing and presented his work nationally and internationally.

Mary Rose Day MA BSc HDPHN RM RGN Dip Management

Mary Rose's nursing experience ranges across diverse areas in acute and community settings as: Development Manager Services for Carers; Public Health Nurse; Discharge Co-ordinator; and Co-ordinator for Continuing Education & Training, before moving into nurse education as a Lecturer at Catherine McAuley School of Nursing & Midwifery, UCC, in 2004. She co-ordinates the Postgraduate Certificate in Nursing in the Community and lectures across postgraduate and undergraduate programmes in nursing.

Research areas include self-neglect in adults and older people, life story work, family carers and community nursing. She has presented papers at international and national conferences in Australia, UK and Ireland and has published in a range of journals.

Patricia Fehin MSc BCL BSc RGN

Patricia has extensive clinical nursing experience gained in the UK and Ireland. She is a Lecturer-Practitioner in nursing, Catherine McAuley School of Nursing & Midwifery, UCC, where she lectures across undergraduate and post-graduate nursing programmes, specifically in care of the older adult. She also has a clinical practice and student support remit within the older people services at St Finbarr's Hospital, Cork.

She was a founding member of the Cork-Kerry Gerontological Nursing Development Group (2001 to 2008) and the All Ireland Gerontological Nursing Association (AIGNA), established in 2009.

Her research areas are the relationship between socio-economic rights and Irish constitutional law, with emphasis on access to healthcare and legal and ethical issues of capacity and the right to refuse life-sustaining medical treatment.

Elizabeth Heffernan MBA MA BSc HDip Educ HDip Healthcare Management, RNT RGN RM

Elizabeth is the Director of Nursing Education at the Kerry Centre of Nurse Education, Tralee General Hospital. She is a part-time lecturer at the Institute of Technology, Tralee.

Following experience in nursing and midwifery at Leeds University Hospital, she held posts in Tralee as: Post-natal Clinical Nurse Manager; Nurse Teacher; and Lecturer in Nursing. She was a steering committee and education sub-group member for the National Clinical Leadership programme (2009 to 2010) and a member of the Kerry Learning Forum.

She supervises MSc nursing research students and has research published on preceptorship. Her other areas of research interest include breastfeeding, education, management and leadership.

Josephine Hegarty PhD MSc BSc RNT RGN

Josephine is Professor of Nursing, working within the Catherine McAuley School of Nursing & Midwifery in UCC. She holds the position of co-director of undergraduate education.

Her research interests have focused on optimising the experience of the cancer journey for patients and their families. Josephine has been a Cochrane Research Fellow and has completed a Cochrane systematic review on watchful waiting *versus* prostatectomy for prostate cancer.

She supervises many PhD and Msc students for their research dissertations. Josephine has published extensively in the international literature.

Patricia Leahy-Warren PhD Msc Bsc PG Public Health RPHN RM RGN

Patricia is Senior Lecturer, Catherine McAuley School of Nursing & Midwifery in UCC.

She has a clinical background in general nursing, midwifery and public health nursing and she held posts, both nationally and internationally, in these areas.

She is the recipient of Health Research Board Research Fellowships for both her Msc (Nursing) and her PhD, which was focused on the concept of first-time motherhood.

She leads the Maternal & Infant Health Research Team within the School and her research interests are maternal care, postnatal depression, social support, maternal parental self-efficacy, breastfeeding, 'kangaroo' care and public health concerns.

John Linehan Msc Bsc RGN RNT

John was Director of Nursing in a Community Hospital and currently is Regional Specialist, Services for Older People for the Health Service Executive – Southern Region. This role is varied and John has been involved in the development of a dementia-specific care unit, preparing a position paper on the future direction of residential care services for people with dementia and in developing a national restraint policy.

He has completed two modules in Dementia Care at Master's Level through Bradford University, United Kingdom (UK) and is trained in using Dementia Care Mapping.

He has published on residential care services for people with dementia in acute care. He plans to contribute further to the development of dementia care services in Ireland.

Lynne Marsh MA MSc BSc

Lynne is a College Lecturer in the Catherine McAuley School of Nursing & Midwifery, UCC and Branch Leader for the BSc Nursing Intellectual Disability programme.

Her teaching and research is focused on nursing in intellectual disability and, through this, she works closely with the COPE Foundation in Cork. Her research interests are health needs of people with intellectual disabilities; parents' experiences of having a child with an intellectual disability; and reusable learning outcomes (RLOs).

Margaret McKiernan MSc BSc PGDip Intensive Care Nursing RGN

Margaret is Assistant Director of Nursing, Nurse Practice Development Co-ordinator in the Mercy University Hospital, Cork.

She has previously worked as Clinical Nurse Manager in Intensive Care at CUH, as clinical facilitator for the post-graduate programme in intensive care and as a clinical nurse in cardiac and intensive care in Cork and Dublin.

Margaret completed a successful application for Health Research Board funding that enabled her full-time release from clinical practice to complete a MSc degree by research.

Helen Mulcahy MSc BSc PGDip PHN RPHN RM RGN

Helen is a College Lecturer and Co-ordinator of the Postgraduate Diploma in Public Health Nursing, Catherine McAuley School of Nursing & Midwifery, UCC.

Helen has over 25 years' experience, both nationally and internationally, in general, midwifery and public health nursing. She has worked in acute and community hospitals as well as primary healthcare. Prior to her current position, she was Assistant Director of Public Health Nursing in Waterford.

Her area of teaching and research expertise includes nurse/client relationships; working with vulnerable families; breastfeeding support; and public health nursing. Her MSc research was supported by a Health Research Board Fellowship. Currently, she is working with a research team on a funded project commissioned by the Health Service Executive, focusing on a review of breastfeeding support services provided by public health nurses.

Brendan Noonan MSc BSc HDip ENT RGN PGDip Teaching and Learning in Higher Education

Brendan is a Lecturer-Practitioner in the Catherine McAuley School of Nursing & Midwifery, UCC. He divides his time between lecturing and working with nursing students in providing direct patient care in the South Infirmary/Victoria University Hospital, Cork.

Brendan has worked as a surgical/ear nose and throat nurse in a variety of hospitals.

He has received funding from the Irish Cancer Society to study the impact of a total laryngectomy from a patient's perspective. Findings from this research and other endeavours have been published and presented nationally and internationally.

He is a member of the national executive committee of the Irish Association for Nurses in Oncology, which promotes continuing nursing education that ultimately aims to improve the care provided to oncology patients.

Elizabeth (Liz) O'Connell MSc BSc PGDip Critical Care Nursing PGDip Teaching and Learning in Higher Education

Liz is a Lecturer-Practitioner at the Catherine McAuley School of Nursing & Midwifery in UCC. She teaches across undergraduate and postgraduate programmes in respiratory, neurosciences and critical care nursing and co-ordinates the clinical component of the Nurse Prescribing Programme.

Her clinical background is in intensive care nursing and, in this area and in neuroscience clinical areas, she works with students in delivering patient care.

She has published in the areas of critical care nursing, haematological nursing, nurse prescribing and the role of the Lecturer-Practitioner. She is currently involved in research on patients who have experienced strokes.

Irene O'Connor RGN RM RNT Dip TQM PGDip CEA MSc

Irene is currently on secondment to the National Fair Deal Taskforce. She led and managed the first project on elder abuse in Ireland. She also was appointed Honorary President of the Irish Association of Directors of Nursing & Midwifery, a position that she held for two years.

She has worked in the UK and Switzerland in surgical and critical care nursing, midwifery, nursing education, and more recently, eldercare. She has presented and published her work nationally.

Eileen Savage PhD MEd BNS RGN RSCN

Eileen is Professor of Nursing at the Catherine McAuley School of Nursing & Midwifery, UCC.

She is actively involved in research and teaching. Her teaching interests are in research methodology, evidence-based practice and children's nursing and healthcare. She leads a research programme on chronic illness management, with a special interest in self-management and family-management. She has conducted a number of funded research projects, and works with national and international collaborators. Her work has been published in the international peer-reviewed literature.

Sandra Swanton MSc BSc RGN

Sandra works in Intellectual Disability Nursing at the COPE Foundation Cork.

She has worked as a Clinical Placement Co-ordinator and, most recently, as a Practice Development Nurse facilitating and supporting staff with practice development initiatives such as: Clinical Audit, Standard-setting, Policy Development and Person-centred Planning. Previous posts include Lecturer in Nursing at UCC and in clinical practice in Ireland and Australia in the field of intellectual disability nursing. She gained experience across a wide range of services including: acute care, residential services for people with multiple and complex disabilities, and an activation day service.

She is an instructor for Manual Handling, Basic Life Support and Cardiac First Response.

She was awarded an All Ireland Research Fellowship from An Bord Altranais and the Northern Ireland Nursing Board, which facilitated her MSc degree research.

Nuala Walshe RGN MN MA Teaching and Learning in Higher Education

Nuala is the Clinical Skills Simulation Resource Centre Manager for the Catherine McAuley School of Nursing & Midwifery, UCC.

She earned a Master's in Nursing at the University of Technology, Sydney, Australia and a Master's in Teaching and Learning at UCC.

Nuala is particularly interested in high-fidelity simulation in nurse education; she has co-authored a number of articles and presented widely on this topic. She has been the recipient of a number of teaching and learning awards at local and national level.

Nuala has a specific interest in patient safety and the factors that impact on patient safety during hospitalisation.

Teresa Wills MSc BSc RGN

Teresa is a College Lecturer in the Catherine McAuley School of Nursing & Midwifery, UCC. She is involved in the delivery and development of both undergraduate and postgraduate nurse education. Teresa co-ordinates the Postgraduate Diploma/ Certificate Programmes in Gerontological Nursing.

Prior to this, she was a clinical placement co-ordinator and nurse tutor in the Bon Secours Hospital, Cork.

She is a member of the Healthy Ageing Research Theme and the ISS21 Ageing Cluster group within the university.

Her research interests include the older adult, obesity, complementary therapies and handwashing. She has published and presented papers at national and international conferences.